THE MAN IN LINCOLN'S NOSE

Funny, Profound, and Quotable Quotes of Screenwriters, Movie Stars, and Moguls

Melinda Corey

and

George Ochoa

A FIRESIDE BOOK · PUBLISHED BY SIMON & SCHUSTER INC.
NEW YORK LONDON TORONTO SYDNEY TOKYO SINGAPORE

FIRESIDE
SIMON & SCHUSTER BUILDING
ROCKEFELLER CENTER
1230 AVENUE OF THE AMERICAS
NEW YORK, NEW YORK 10020

COPYRIGHT © 1990 BY BLUE CLIFF EDITIONS, INC.

FIRESIDE AND COLOPHON ARE REGISTERED TRADEMARKS
OF SIMON & SCHUSTER INC.

DESIGNED BY BONNI LEON
MANUFACTURED IN THE UNITED STATES OF AMERICA

10 9 8 7 6 5 4 3 2 1 PBK.

LIBRARY OF CONGRESS CATALOGING IN PUBLICATION DATA
THE MAN IN LINCOLN'S NOSE: FUNNY, PROFOUND, AND QUOTABLE
QUOTES OF SCREENWRITERS, MOVIE STARS, AND MOGULS/ [COMPILED BY]
MELINDA COREY AND GEORGE OCHOA.
    P. CM.
  "A FIRESIDE BOOK."
   1. MOTION PICTURES—HUMOR. 2. MOTION PICTURE ACTORS AND
ACTRESSES—QUOTATIONS. 3. MOTION PICTURE PRODUCERS AND
DIRECTORS—QUOTATIONS. 4. SCREENWRITERS—
QUOTATIONS. I. COREY, MELINDA. II. OCHOA, GEORGE.
PN1994.9.M35 1990
791.43—DC20
                                89-26213
                                  CIP

ISBN 0-671-68172-9 PBK.

TO
OUR
PARENTS

Acknowledgments

The authors would like to thank Jason Shulman and Malaika Adero for their support in bringing this book to completion.

Our original title, you know, was The Man in Lincoln's Nose. *Couldn't use it, though. They also wouldn't let us shoot people on Mount Rushmore. Can't deface a national monument. And it's a pity, too, because I had a wonderful shot in mind of Cary Grant hiding in Lincoln's nose and having a sneezing fit.*

—*Alfred Hitchcock on* North by Northwest

A Note on Organization

This book is divided into twenty-three sections related to the people and activities surrounding moviemaking. Within each of these sections, quotes are arranged in two ways. In most cases, quotes run chronologically, from past to present. In some cases, however, as with a series of quotes on a single film, we have strung together quotes of varying dates. This is meant to provide a more unified view of the chronology of a particular movie.

Contents

Introduction: Memories and Movies

I saw my first movie when I was six. It was John Stahl's *Imitation of Life*, with Claudette Colbert and Louise Beavers. All I remember of it is a shot of an ad for the pancake mix that made Colbert's character famous and the smell of the sofa where my mother and I lay. *The Sound of Music* recalls a high balcony and a desire to sew our living room draperies into play clothes. When I was sixteen, I was moved by the performances in *The Last Picture Show*, but what I remember most vividly are my parents' disgruntled gasps as the bed creaked under Timothy Bottoms's and Cloris Leachman's clumsy embrace. Our family never saw another R-rated movie together.

Memories of movies are of necessity both incomplete and embellished. If we can't recall what we ate for lunch last Tuesday, how can we grasp a world presented to us in twenty-four frames per second? And if movie watching is a social experience, how can we not be affected by the surroundings —the satisfying *whoosh* of the draperies revealing the screen, the amiable friction of the seat cushion, the benign titillation of the smell of someone else's popcorn butter drifting down-screen?

Just as we have memories of moviegoing, moviemakers have memories of their experiences. Like ours, their memories are both less and more at the same time. They don't capture the experiences completely, but they are all we have.

Memories are the main ingredient of *The Man in Lincoln's Nose*. There are 875 memories in this book. Some date from the time of the movie's creation; others come decades afterward. Some quotes, from in-studio memoranda and personal letters, have the appearance of authenticity; others, from interviews years later of stars whose minds have narrowed or whose egos have ballooned, raise an eyebrow. But who can determine what is true? One of the makers of the 1932 classic *Scarface* was inspired by the Borgia family to cast the brother-sister relationship in an incestuous light. But which one? Director Howard Hawks claims he told screenwriter Ben Hecht, "Well, Ben, I've got an idea that the Borgia family is living in Chicago today. See, our Borgia is Al Capone, and his sister does the same incest thing as Lucretia Borgia." But according to screenwriter John Lee Mahin, "*Ben* said that to *Hawks*. I heard him say that. The Borgias have always been Ben's favorite characters. Howard, bless his heart, probably knew who they were, but I think he looked them up in the encyclopedia."

Which story of *The African Queen* should we believe: Bogart's—"Katie starts out as a missionary, but after going downriver with me, she ends up as a woman," or Hepburn's—". . . I start out as a woman and end up as a missionary trying to save Bogart"? And who can define Harry Cohn, the much-hated studio head of Columbia Pictures? To screenwriter Sidney Sheldon, he was a "bastard," while colleague James Cain felt that even though Cohn "could growl or raise hell . . . the writer or actor . . . could get along with him." Director Elia Kazan said only that "Cohn wanted to be the biggest bug in the manure pile." Cohn's own words suggest a more vulnerable side: "If I sell the company, who's going to call me on the telephone?"

Incomplete as they are alone, together these thoughts create a picture—of an actor, a director, a film, a time. They don't provide the definitive version of the behind-the-scenes world of moviemaking, but it doesn't matter. As the newspaper editor in *The Man Who Shot Liberty Valance* reminds us, "When the legend becomes fact, print the legend."

—Melinda Corey

Actors

"You should play Hamlet."
"To hell with them small towns. I'll take New York."

> John Barrymore and
> Jimmy Durante
> *circa 1930s*

As I see it, Eddie, the whole fault lies in the fact that you want to be a writer. By this I mean that you want to put your views into whatever subject we purchase rather than to accept the views of the men I engage here who are specialists at a high salary in this specific work.

> Darryl F. Zanuck answering
> script criticism by Edward G.
> Robinson
> *1932*

"Mr. Hawks, just why do you think I would be any good in this picture [*Twentieth Century*]?"
"It's the story of the greatest ham in the world, and God knows you fit that."
"I'll do the picture."

> John Barrymore and
> Howard Hawks
> *circa 1933*

He brought in Walter Brennan, and I looked at him and laughed. I said, "Mr. Brennan, did they give you some lines?" He said, "Yeah." . . . I said, "Do you want to read them?" And he said, "With or without?" I said, "With or without what?" He said, "Teeth."

> Howard Hawks and
> Walter Brennan
>> *circa 1934*

WHAT DO YOU THINK ABOUT RONALD COLMAN FOR THE LEAD?

> David O. Selznick on *Gone
> With the Wind*
>> *1936*

"You've written a scene here for Gary Cooper that he couldn't speak in a million years."
"You mean I should stick to 'yep' and 'nope'? "
"Exactly."

> Goldwyn studio executive and
> Charles Bennett, screenwriter,
> on *The Adventures of Marco
> Polo*
>> *circa 1937*

Larry [Olivier's] silent action and reactions [in *Rebecca*] become slower as his dialogue becomes faster each day. . . . [The scene about giving a ball] is played as though he were deciding whether or not to run for President instead of whether or not to give a ball.

> David O. Selznick
>> *1939*

A lean, stringy, dark-faced piece of electricity walked out on the screen and he had me. I believed my own story again.

> John Steinbeck on Henry
> Fonda's performance in *The
> Grapes of Wrath*
> *circa 1940*

Why'd you use a midget? That man you used in the test, he's a midget.

> MGM studio executive on
> viewing Alan Ladd's first
> screen test
> *circa 1940s*

I'm sure I'd be damn good as Little Lord Fauntleroy, but who would pay ten cents to see it?

> Boris Karloff on typecasting
> *circa 1940s*

I don't have to do any more motion pictures. I can get out of the industry. I'm a cowboy at heart.

> Joel McCrea, turning down
> the lead in *The Devil Is a
> Woman*
> *circa 1940s*

I saw the boy in her [Stella Adler's] classrooms, and the genius Stella was talking about was not apparent to the naked eye. He looked to me like a kid who delivers groceries.

> Clifford Odets on
> Marlon Brando
> *circa 1940s*

We have been ejected from MGM and are now conducting what little business we have in a barnlike building catercornered from the Bank of America. It's very convenient, especially for Chico, who now has only to cross the street to stop payment on the checks he's written the night before.

> Groucho Marx at the start of
> his temporary retirement from
> movies
>
> *1941*

I am sorry to have to say that I don't see what we could do with Gregory Peck. . . . He photographs like Abe Lincoln, but if he had a great personality, I don't think it comes through in these tests.

> David O. Selznick
>
> *1941*

CONFIDENTIALLY, IMPOSSIBLE SIGN UP [JOHN] GARFIELD AFTER HE MAKES ONE MORE PICTURE FOR US. HE HAS FORGOTTEN DAYS WHEN I PICKED HIM UP WHEN MAKING SIX BITS WEEKLY. . . . DON'T WANT TROUBLE WITH HIM WHEN WE MAKING LAST ONE, AS HE NO PUSHOVER.

> Jack L. Warner
>
> *1945*

I understand you don't think acting is a *worthy* enough profession. Don't you *realize* you're moving millions of people, shaping their lives, giving them a sense of exaltation. . . . What other profession has that *power* or can be so important?

... Acting is among the oldest and noblest professions in the world, young man.

> Lionel Barrymore to James
> Stewart on the set of *It's a
> Wonderful Life,* when Stewart
> was thinking of leaving the
> acting business
>
> *1946*

If he'd have lived, they'd have discovered he wasn't a legend.

> Humphrey Bogart on
> James Dean
>
> *circa 1950s*

The name's got to go.

> Harry Cohn on meeting
> Jack Lemmon
>
> *circa 1950s*

I've made a career, in a sense, of playing sons of bitches.

> Kirk Douglas
>
> *circa 1950s*

Quick transformation from one character to another [in *Kind Hearts and Coronets*] has a disturbing effect. I had to ask myself from time to time: "Which one am I now?" ... It would have been quite disastrous to have faced the camera in the makeup of the suffragette and spoken like the admiral.

> Alec Guinness on the
> difficulties of playing eight
> characters in one film
>
> *1952*

All great actors are really character actors.

Orson Welles

1957

I would like to be the world's greatest character lover.

Dustin Hoffman

1968

I was afraid to say, "Spencer, you're a great actor." He'd only say, "Now what the hell kind of thing is that to come out with?" He wanted to know it; he *needed* to know it. But he didn't want you to *say* it, just *think* it.

Stanley Kramer on Spencer
Tracy in *Inherit the Wind*
circa 1959

In trying to understand the man I had married, I once questioned his psychiatrist on the subject of "mooning." I was told that baboons display their buttocks to other baboons as an act of submission. In Homo sapiens (or in those few who engage in such practice), the design would seem to be the reverse.

Anna Kashfi Brando
circa 1960s

He was good in anything. Played himself but he played the character. . . . People just liked him.

John Ford on James Stewart
circa 1960s

[James] Stewart is a perfect Hitchcock hero because he is Everyman in bizarre situations.

> Alfred Hitchcock
> *circa 1960s*

One doesn't direct Gary Grant; one simply puts him in front of a camera.

> Alfred Hitchcock
> *circa 1960s*

[He had] a sadness about the human condition. He had a kind of eighteenth-century, Alexander Pope nature. I think he would have made a superb Gatsby. His life reflected Gatsby's sense of being an outsider.

> Joseph L. Mankiewicz on
> Humphrey Bogart
> *circa 1960s*

In *Duel at Diablo* he [Sidney Poitier] did little more than hold James Garner's hat—and this after he had won the Academy Award. What white romantic actor would take a part like that?

> Clifford Mason, playwright
> *circa 1960s*

I dredged up "Karloff" from Russian ancestors on my mother's side and I picked "Boris" out of the chilly, Canadian air.

> William Henry Pratt on his
> stage name
> *circa 1960s*

ACTORS

People used to ask Spencer Tracy, "Don't you ever get tired of playing Spencer Tracy?" An' he'd say, "Who the hell do you *want* me to play!?"

James Stewart

circa 1960s

An' *that's* the thing—that's the great thing about the movies. . . . After you *learn*—and if you're good and Gawd helps ya and you're lucky enough to have a personality that comes across—then what you're doing is, you're giving people little . . . little, tiny pieces of *time* . . . that they never forget.

James Stewart

circa 1960s

Both Laurence Olivier and I detest our own noses. They tend to give our faces a comic appearance, whereas we both have a strong desire to play mainly dramatic roles. . . . For all normal uses, my own nose is quite pleasant and fairly decorative. It stopped growing, however, when I was about ten years old. Thus it is violently unsuitable for roles such as Lear, Macbeth, and Othello.

Orson Welles

circa 1960s

Argh! Lancaster—he's a *cowboy*, no?

Luchino Visconti on the
suggestion that Burt Lancaster
star in *The Leopard*

1963

We're geniuses. We're both geniuses, Hoppy.

> Jack Nicholson with Dennis
> Hopper on a day off during
> the filming of *Easy Rider*
> *circa 1968*

You'll never know how lonely those years were for me when I was the only black star out there. Now I walk down the street and see Jim Brown's name big on the marquees, and I feel good.

> Sidney Poitier on the growing
> acceptance of black actors in
> the late 1960s
> *1969*

"What's your name?"
"Cary Grant."
"You don't look like Cary Grant."
"I know—nobody does."

> Cary Grant and a reser-
> vation clerk at the Beverly
> Wilshire Hotel gala honoring
> John Ford
> *1971*

I don't want any funny lines; I just want to keep leaping after the girls and squeezing that horn.

> Dustin Hoffman on his desire
> to play Harpo Marx
> *1971*

There's too much pretentious nonsense talked about the artistic problems of making pictures. I've never had a god-damn artistic problem in my life, never, and I've worked with the best of them. John Ford isn't exactly a bum, is he? Yet he never gave me any manure about art. He just made movies, and that's what I do. . . . In fact, I don't even call myself an actor. I'm a *re-actor*. I listen to what the other guy is saying, and I re-act to it. That's the John Wayne method.

> John Wayne
> *circa 1971*

I doubt if he knows how good he is.

> Marlon Brando on Robert De
> Niro in *The Godfather, Part II*
> *circa 1974*

I didn't want to do an imitation of Brando, but I wanted to make it believable that I could be him as a young man. It was like a mathematical problem.

> Robert De Niro
> *circa 1974*

My theory was that I could foul up my career just as well as somebody else could foul it up for me, so why not try it?

> Clint Eastwood on forming his
> own production company
> *1974*

I'd seen [Gene] Kelly in New York and he said: "Do you want to test me, because I'm not a handsome guy." I said: "No, you're not going to look any different if you do a test."

> Arthur Freed on discovering
> Gene Kelly
> *1974*

After that picture [*The Fugitive Kind*] the only way I'd work with Marlon Brando is if he were in rear projection.

Joanne Woodward

1974

He's, sort of, very shiny, and he has a very white aura that kind of glows and shines. . . . He always grants people being-ness, so to speak. He grants them their-ness. He grants them you-ness and me-ness, and a lot of people don't do that.

Karen Black on
Jack Nicholson

circa 1975

Then he [Jack Nicholson] made *Five Easy Pieces*. Well, he's a major fuckin' star now, and I'm in the toilet.

Bruce Dern

circa 1975

I think I'm a little bit more like Lenin, and he [Jack Nichol-son]'s sort of like the czar. . . . He loves the fame, the wealth, the limousines driving him to and from. Whereas I get terribly embarrassed riding in a limousine.

Dennis Hopper

circa 1975

When they broke, I cornered [William] Devane, who is bright and very articulate, and I told him how wonderfully he had done and asked what it was like rehearsing with Laurence Olivier [for *Marathon Man*]. "It doesn't matter," Devane replied. ". . . When the camera starts to roll, he'll give me a little of this, he'll give me a little of that, and you'll never know I'm in the movie. That's Olivier, man."

William Goldman,
screenwriter
circa 1975

If you look back through history, the people who've been the strongest in film were people who could express a lot by holding certain things in reserve so that the audience is curious to find out what the reserve is.

Clint Eastwood
1979

I decided to become an actor because I was failing in school and I needed the credits.

Dustin Hoffman
1979

The uglies.

Jack Warner, Jr., on Hoffman, Streisand, and other post-1960 actors
circa 1980

I was used to his [Alan Ladd] being top banana, and we both felt the Jimmy Dean role was a secondary part. It didn't turn out that way.

Sue Carol, Ladd's agent and wife, on why he turned down the role of Jett Rink in *Giant*
circa 1980s

When I was in *Over the Edge,* someone told me I was like Brando. I didn't take that as a compliment. I thought he was a fat old man—the only thing I'd seen him in was *The Godfather.* Then I saw *A Streetcar Named Desire.*

> Matt Dillon
>
> *1982*

If ever I had a message to get across, you'll find it in *Bronco Billy.*

> Clint Eastwood
>
> *circa 1982*

I had trouble the first day with Bogart. I think I grabbed him by the lapels and pushed his head up against the wall and said, "Look, Bogey. I tell you how to get tough, but don't get tough with me." He said, "I won't." Everything was fine from that time on.

> Howard Hawks on Bogart in
> *To Have and Have Not*
>
> *1982*

There are lots of actors with the title "Sir." . . . Laurence [Olivier]'s the first and will probably be the *only* actor to be made a lord. . . . Being a lord is like being a Rockefeller and being a sir is just rich.

> Michael Caine
>
> *1983*

First of all I choose the great ones, and if none of those come, I choose the mediocre ones, and if they don't come—I choose the ones that are going to pay the rent.

> Michael Caine on
> selecting roles
> *1983*

There is no difference between doing this kind of film [*Return of the Jedi*] and playing *King Lear*. The actor's job is exactly the same: Dress up and pretend.

> Harrison Ford
> *circa 1983*

I'm not crazy, but I think everybody else is.

> Peter O'Toole
> *1983*

Why don't you try *acting*? It's much easier.

> Laurence Olivier to Dustin
> Hoffman, on Hoffman's
> intense acting style in
> *Marathon Man*
> *1983*

I guess it was because I really remember how much Dad [Lloyd Bridges] got off on the success of *Sea Hunt*.

> Jeff Bridges on why he
> became an actor
> *circa 1984*

To hear Kirk [Douglas] tell it, he was the poorest, most miserable child that ever lived. I think it would annihilate him to meet someone who was poorer than he says he was. He wouldn't be able to believe it.

Anne Douglas

circa 1984

Some actors are unable to separate make-believe from reality. I never thought I was Spartacus. Someone said to me, "I saw you in *Lust for Life,* and, my God, you were so lost in the role." I said, "No, *you* were lost in the role. That's my job."

Kirk Douglas

circa 1984

Let's just say he prefers it.

Harrison Ford on why he refers to Sir Alec Guinness as "Sir Alec"

circa 1984

Until I decide how a character walks, nothing happens.

Alec Guinness

1985

Gaining the weight was very depressing. It's the last time I'll ever do that.

Robert De Niro on playing Al Capone in *The Untouchables*

1987

I don't like that *Gone With the Wind*–type of acting. Clark Gable was a good actor, but he always played himself.

> Robert De Niro
>
> *1987*

There is a period when you're no longer Lawrence of Arabia and when one can no longer hit home runs as often as one would wish to.

> Peter O'Toole
>
> *1987*

In one scene [in *Bloody Mama*] he [Robert De Niro] had to drive us in this car. . . . Suddenly we're careening around this field, and it's like he's out of control at the wheel. I whispered, "Bobby, do you know how to drive?" and he grinned. "Are you kidding? I'm from New York. Why would I know how to drive?"

> Shelley Winters
>
> *1987*

A lot of people thought Bob [Redford] was wooden in *Out of Africa*. I didn't. I thought he was subtle—and just right. But then I'm the worst one to ask. I had a big crush on him.

> Meryl Streep
>
> *circa 1988*

[H]e's a kid off a Wheaties box.

> Oliver Stone on Tom Cruise
>
> *1989*

I always thought I was an actor pretending to be a movie star.

Tom Cruise

1989

When I drove through the studio gate, and the thrill was gone, I knew it was time to quit.

James Cagney

circa 1960s

Actresses

Harry, forget Stanwyck. She's not an actress; she's a porcupine.

> Frank Capra on his first
> impression of Barbara
> Stanwyck
>> *circa 1930*

Underneath that red-gold hair is a very level head and a sense of humor not often found in beautiful women.

> Ernst Lubitsch on Jeanette
> MacDonald
>> *circa 1930s*

Ye gods, that horse face!

> RKO executives on first seeing
> screen tests of Katharine
> Hepburn
>> *circa 1931*

She stole everything but the cameras.

> George Raft on Mae West in
> *Night After Night*
>> *circa 1932*

She had what it took to make the widow merry; without her, it would have been a very sad widow indeed.

> Irving Thalberg on Jeanette
> MacDonald in *The Merry
> Widow*
> .
> *circa 1934*

D'ja see her *face?* Half of it's angel, and the other half horse.

> Harry Cohn on Jean Arthur
> *circa 1935*

We have lost our enthusiasm for a production of *Anna Karenina* as your next picture. I personally feel that audiences are waiting to see you in a smart, modern picture and that to do a heavy Russian drama on the heels of so many ponderous, similar films . . . would prove to be a mistake.

> David O. Selznick to Greta
> Garbo
> *1935*

Would you *please* speak to Marlene [Dietrich] about the fact that her hair is getting so much attention and is being coiffed to such a degree that all reality is lost.

> David O. Selznick to Richard
> Boleslawski, director of *The
> Garden of Allah*
> *1936*

Where the average glamour girl fears to tread, Bette Davis steps in and "takes over." We should let her stay that way and under no conditions try to make a "Garbo" or "Kay Francis" out of her. Bette Davis is a female Cagney and if we give her the right parts, we are going to have a star that will pay off the interest on the bonds every year.

> S. Charles Enfield, director of
> publicity and advertising,
> Warner Bros.
>
> *1937*

"You know this part was practically written for me. I *am* Scarlett O'Hara. So what's the matter?"

"All right, I'll tell you. I just can't imagine Clark Gable chasing you for ten years."

> Katharine Hepburn and David
> O. Selznick
>
> *circa 1930s*

Ingrid Berriman is a lot better, but certainly this is no name that you would go out of the way to tack on to a personality either.

> David O. Selznick on possible
> stage names for Ingrid
> Bergman
>
> *1939*

I NOTE BERGMAN IS 69½ INCHES TALL. IS IT POSSIBLE SHE IS ACTUALLY THIS HIGH, AND DO YOU THINK WE WILL HAVE TO USE STEPLADDERS WITH LESLIE HOWARD?

> David O. Selznick on the two
> principals in *Intermezzo*
>
> *1939*

Ann Rutherford . . . told me something which might be the basis of some excellent publicity, which is that all the girls she knows are letting their eyebrows grow in as a result of Bergman's unplucked eyebrows.

David O. Selznick

1939

If a face like Ingrid Bergman's looks at you as though you're adorable, everybody does. You don't have to act very much.

Humphrey Bogart

circa 1940s

Where the hell is that new name for Phyllis Walker? . . . Personally, I would like to decide on Jennifer and get a one-syllable last name that has some rhythm to it and that is easy to remember.

David O. Selznick on the actress who became Jennifer Jones

1942

[I] will try, as much as possible, to talk him [Howard Hawks] out of Betty Bacall.

Steve Trilling, Warner Bros. executive assistant, on *To Have and Have Not*

1943

Give the girl [Lauren Bacall] at least three or four additional scenes with Bogart of the insolent and provocative nature that she had in *To Have and Have Not*. You see, Jack, in *To Have and Have Not* Bacall was more insolent than Bogart and this very insolence endeared her in both the public's and the critics' mind when the picture appeared.

> Charles K. Feldman, agent, to
> Jack L. Warner on *The Big
> Sleep*
>
> 1945

"Is she a Californian?"
"No. She's a lady."

> Michael Powell, British
> director, and Alfred Hitchcock
> on Kim Hunter
>
> *circa 1945*

You mean I'm related to a president of the United States?

> Marilyn Monroe on the
> ancestry of her mother, née
> Monroe, from whom she took
> her stage name
>
> *circa 1940s*

Elizabeth Taylor is a nervous, high-strung youngster, whose condition has caused her to absent herself fairly frequently from the pictures which she [has] worked in. . . . This has been aggravated somewhat recently by a natural condition in girls of her age.

> Phil Friedman, Warner Bros.
> casting director, on casting the
> fourteen-year-old Taylor in
> *Life with Father*
>
> 1946

Tighter, Miss Head, tighter.

> Elizabeth Taylor to costume
> designer Edith Head, on her
> wardrobe
> *1949*

"Katie starts out as a missionary, but after going downriver with me, she ends up as a woman."
"I'd say I start out as a woman and end up as a missionary trying to save Bogart."

> Humphrey Bogart and
> Katharine Hepburn on the
> plot of *The African Queen*
> *circa 1951*

Yes, there was something special about me, and I knew what it was. I was the kind of girl they found dead in a hall bedroom with an empty bottle of sleeping pills in her hand.

> Marilyn Monroe
> *circa 1950s*

[Audrey Hepburn] is like a salmon swimming upstream. She can do it with very small bozooms. . . . This girl single-handed may make bozooms a thing of the past. The director will not have to invent shots where the girl leans way forward for a glass of Scotch and soda.

> Billy Wilder
> *circa 1950s*

I called attention to her long neck, so that people began to describe her as "swanlike" and "graceful" instead of "gangly."

> Edith Head on Audrey
> Hepburn
> *circa 1980*

I always thought Mae West was the most famous figure in drama, and she had the figure to prove it.

> Tennessee Williams
> *circa 1950s*

Very few girls could jump in my lap and say "Please love me" the way she did.

> Frank Sinatra on Shirley
> MacLaine in *Some Came
> Running*
> *circa 1958*

I like joy; I want to be joyous; I want to have fun on the set; I want to wear beautiful clothes and look pretty. I want to smile, and I want to make people laugh. And that's all I want. I like it. I like being happy. I want to make others happy.

> Doris Day
> *1962*

It's amazing to find so many people who I thought really know me could have thought that *Sunset [Boulevard]* was autobiographical. I've got nobody floating in my swimming pool.

> Gloria Swanson
> *1964*

Cagney used to say that I was the most naive sophisticate he'd ever seen in his life, 'cause he knew me very well. He knew I was a shy kind of a gal, and that, playing all these whore ladies, I didn't know what they did, even.

Joan Blondell

1970

I fell in love with Stanwyck, and had I not been more in love with [my wife] Lucille Reyburn, I would have asked Barbara to marry me.

Frank Capra

1971

In *Dr. Jekyll and Mr. Hyde* Lana Turner was cast as the little barmaid and I was to play Dr. Jekyll's fiancée. I went to the director and said I was so fed up playing the same part over and over again. I said I'd like to play the barmaid. He said that with my face I couldn't do that. I said, "What do you know about my face? Let's do a little test." ... [T]he test turned out very well and we switched the parts. I'm sure Lana was just as happy as I was, because she was always playing barmaids!

Ingrid Bergman

1972

In the film [*All About Eve*] I stood backstage watching Anne Baxter play Eve, and then, twenty years later, I stood backstage in real life watching Anne play Margo [in the musical version *Applause*]. ... I felt very, *very old* that day.

Bette Davis

1974

I always thought that Judy would come back. I thought she was made out of iron. She came back so many times. And in the interview I gave [*New York Times* critic] Bosley Crowther before Judy had passed away, I said: "Judy will come back."

Arthur Freed, producer, on
Judy Garland
1974

The first time I have seen Joan Crawford . . . was the time when the shoulders didn't exist anymore in fashion—it was off—and she came to see me and I said, "Well, she's still wearing those pads." No, it was her shoulders. She had square shoulders, like this. . . . I thought, "My God, those are the [designer] Adrian shoulders." I thought Adrian had made them, but they were hers.

Jean Louis, costume designer
1977

Elizabeth Taylor, weigh[ing] 140 pounds, with twenty-two changes of wardrobe by Shariff, living in an $85,000 beach house, is not a young woman penniless, with a bastard child, trying to be an artist.

Dalton Trumbo, screenwriter,
on *The Sandpiper*
circa 1978

He [Howard Hawks] wanted me to drive into the hills, find some quiet spot, and read aloud. He felt it most important to keep the voice in a low register. Mine started off low, but what Howard didn't like and explained to me was, "If you notice, Betty, when a woman gets excited or emotional, she tends to raise her voice. Now there is nothing more unattractive than screeching. I want you to train your voice in such a way that even if you have a scene like that, your voice will remain low." I found a spot on Mulholland Drive and proceeded to read *The Robe* aloud, keeping my voice lower and louder than normal. If anyone ever passed by, they would have found me a candidate for the asylum. Who sat on mountaintops in cars reading books aloud to the canyons?

> Lauren Bacall recalling her preparation for her screen debut in *To Have and Have Not*
>
> *1979*

She is a still picture—unchangeable.

> Louise Brooks on Greta Garbo
> *circa 1980*

I get sent lots and lots of heroines and nice-girl parts. You know. There's some man who moves the plot, and his sidekick is a girl who has one nude scene and is vulnerable and kind of funny at times . . . the kind of thing you just never want to see again. I want to do something gritty, something real funny, a real smelly part.

> Meryl Streep
> *1980*

It's better to keep working, no matter what. There are no small parts—just small actors.

> Mae Clarke, costar of *The Public Enemy*
> *circa 1980s*

I put on my own bra and put Kleenex over the seams and I went out and Howard [Hughes] took a look and said, "Okay," and went right ahead and he never knew the difference.

> Jane Russell on how she avoided having to wear an uncomfortable seamless bra of Hughes's design in *The Outlaw*
>
> *circa 1980s*

I want to play leading roles, and I only have—what?—fourteen or fifteen years to do that. . . . And if you want to fit a couple of babies into that schedule as well, you've got to pick your parts with great care.

> Meryl Streep
>
> *1981*

In the case of Geraldine Page, she didn't move well, I thought, as the movie star she was playing [in *Sweet Bird of Youth*]. So I asked her to go watch a movie for me—I had it run for her. It was *A Stolen Life*, where Bette Davis played two parts. . . . [Geraldine] came back to the set and she said, "Don't say *anything*. That bitch can walk *away* from the camera and look like a star. I know what you mean. Don't worry." She was marvelous. She came down the stairs—like a movie star.

> Richard Brooks
>
> *1982*

If Ginger [Rogers] was having trouble with a scene, she always said, "There's something radically wrong with this scene." It took us a couple of pictures to realize that when

Ginger said this, it meant that she was not prepared and doubtless had been on the town the night before.

> Allan Scott, screenwriter, on
> the filming of *Top Hat*
> *circa 1985*

The only power an actor has is the ability to say no.

> Kathleen Turner on turning
> down roles
> *1986*

The only one who could have done it better is me.

> Barbara Stanwyck to Kathleen
> Turner on her performance in
> *Body Heat*
> *circa 1981*

I gazed at her and wondered whether I would go mad with jealousy as I compared our ages—our skin—our hair—our natures.

> Katharine Hepburn on Lauren
> Bacall during the filming of
> *The African Queen*
> *circa 1987*

She always looks like she has a secret.

> Michael Douglas on Glenn
> Close
> *1987*

Acting doesn't come any better than that. I've heard it from everybody from Brando to . . . Chi Chi Rodriguez.

> Jack Nicholson on Anjelica
> Huston in *Prizzi's Honor*
> *circa 1989*

Animals and Animation

It is an axiom of screen comedy that a Shetland pony must never be put in an undignified position. People don't like it. You can take any kind of liberties with a donkey . . . but not a pony. You might as well show Santa Claus being mistreated.

Mack Sennett

1918

You know this is only a temporary job, Les. I don't know what's going to happen.

Walt Disney hiring animator
Les Clark for his fledgling
studio

1927

Mortimer is a horrible name for a mouse!

Lillian Disney on her
husband's original name for
his cartoon rodent

1928

It has been decided that since the talking pictures have come into their own, particularly with this organization, that the making of any animal pictures, such as we have in the past with Rin Tin Tin, is not in keeping with the policy that has been adopted by us for talking pictures, very obviously, of course, because dogs don't talk.

P. A. Chase, Warner Bros.
executive
1929

It is saddening to see Popeye, like a Hun from the north, threatening the more cultured supremacy of Mickey, Minnie, and the intelligent and devoted Pluto.

William De Mille, director, on
a poll showing that children
preferred Popeye the Sailor
Man to Mickey Mouse
1935

He seldom loses his temper. This makes him a good foil for the hot-headed duck.

Ted Sears, Disney story
department head, on Goofy
and Donald
1935

The only star at MGM is Leo the Lion.

Sign on MGM Vice President
Eddie Mannix's desk
circa 1940s

The same soulful eyes, the same beaky face, the same trick of falling into pantomime when at a loss for words.

> Disney Studio animator on the
> resemblances between Walt
> Disney and Mickey Mouse
> *1949*

He put us up in our own little shack . . . in some old dressing room or toilet or something, a little cottage sort of thing. We called it Termite Terrace. And he was smart; he didn't disturb us.

> Tex Avery on how Leon
> Schlesinger set up the
> animation department at
> Warner Bros.
> *circa 1950s*

Gee, it floored 'em! . . . It got such a laugh that we said, "Boy, we'll do that every chance we get."

> Tex Avery on the first time an
> audience heard Bugs Bunny
> say, "What's up, Doc?"
> *circa 1950s*

I hope we never lose sight of one fact . . . that this was all started by a mouse.

> Walt Disney
> *circa 1960s*

[Producer Merian C. Cooper] said to me that he'd had an idea for a film in mind. The only thing he'd tell me was that it was going to have the "tallest leading man in Hollywood." Well, naturally, I thought of Clark Gable . . . and when the script came I was *absolutely appalled*!

> Fay Wray on the making of
> *King Kong*
> *circa 1960s*

We had to do more retakes for human actors than for Trigger.

> Roy Rogers
> *circa 1966*

As you know, it came out at a time when the permissive film was becoming the "in" thing. If you didn't have nudity in a picture, nobody wanted to know. A naked dinosaur just wasn't outrageous enough.

> Ray Harryhausen, stop-motion
> animator, on why the dinosaur
> film *The Valley of Gwangi*
> was not more successful
> *circa 1974*

I just don't know. After all, it's only a shark story.

> Steven Spielberg considering
> whether to take on *Jaws*
> *circa 1974*

We talked with one distinguished action director, but the negotiations faded out. He kept talking about "the whale."

> David Brown on the search for
> a director for *Jaws*
> *circa 1975*

THE MAN IN LINCOLN'S NOSE

If anything, Nissa was afraid of *her*!

> Howard Hawks on whether
> Katharine Hepburn was afraid
> of the leopard Nissa in
> *Bringing Up Baby*
> *circa 1975*

I made Emma [a snake in *The Lady Eve*] a nice diamond necklace from a jeweled buckle, hoping it would fit when it came time to shoot the scenes. . . . The only problem was that it was the hibernating season for snakes and Emma just wanted to sleep, so she proceeded to shed her skin in the middle of production. . . . We finally had to let her do scenes without the necklace, one of my few costuming failures.

> Edith Head
> *circa 1980*

I was strongly advised against shooting with an animal.

> Clint Eastwood on *Every*
> *Which Way but Loose*
> *circa 1984*

I was the one signing the checks.

> Clint Eastwood on how he
> maintained his authority with
> the orangutan in *Every Which*
> *Way but Loose*
> *circa 1978*

[Cecil B.] De Mille, when he was looking for an ending to *Reap the Wild Wind*, said . . . "This is no good. For God's sake, we've got to find an ending." . . . [I]n my bath, in the morning of the following day, I said to myself, "What's wrong with a giant squid?" . . . The following day, I came in and I acted out the entire sequence for De Mille. "Here's John Wayne and Ray Milland out to kill each other . . . and here comes the giant squid!" I played the giant squid. At the end of it, De Mille sat there completely mesmerized. Then he just said, "Charles. Wonderful. In *Technicolor.*"

> Charles Bennett
>
> *circa 1985*

Think of this as a *National Geographic* special on this fly-fusion creature.

> David Cronenberg on *The Fly*
> 1986

[N]eck is [Tex] Avery; body is Disney. Lower face is Warner Bros.

> Richard Williams, animation
> director, writing notes on
> Roger Rabbit
>
> *circa 1986*

A cartoon is the language of dreams—as elastic as time is compressed. When you draw a cartoon, you draw a dream and you have the luxury of having total control over the elements.

> Richard Williams, animation
> director on *Who Framed
> Roger Rabbit?*
> 1988

Censorship

[A] business pure and simple . . . not to be regarded as part of the press of the country or as organs of public opinion.

> Supreme Court ruling
> allowing the censorship of
> movies
> *1915*

At Hollywood is a colony of these people where debauchery, riotous living, drunkenness, ribaldry, dissipation, free love seem to be conspicuous. . . . From these sources our young people gain much of their views of life, inspiration, and education. Rather a poor source, is it not? It looks as if censorship is needed, does it not?

> United States senator to
> Congress
> *1922*

[The only way] to curb the evil influence of evil pictures was to have the pictures made right . . . at the source of production.

> Martin Quigley, cocreator of
> the Production Code, on the
> code's first purpose
> *1937*

Screw the Hays Office [enforcer of the Production Code]. Start the picture and make it as realistic, as exciting, as grisly as possible.

> Howard Hughes to Howard
> Hawks on *Scarface*
> *circa 1931*

Every state had its own censors, and Pennsylvania was the toughest. Whenever anybody took a scene that was the least bit off, everybody would yell: "It won't be shown in Pennsylvania!" But we battled on. Sometimes we'd take maybe six or seven risqué scenes, hoping they'd leave two.

> Raoul Walsh
> *circa 1975*

We must put brassieres on Joan Blondell and make her cover up her breasts because, otherwise, we are going to have these pictures stopped in a lot of places.

> Jack L. Warner on viewing
> *Convention City*
> *1933*

At last [Will H.] Hays has something more effective as a weapon. Yesterday he could only seek to persuade. Today he can demand.

> Robert H. Cochrane,
> executive vice president of
> Universal Pictures, on the
> newly formed Production
> Code Administration
> *1934*

The [Production] Code is a liberal document. Note, for example, that it does not forbid the comic treatment even of sacred subjects, such as a wedding, if properly done for pure entertainment. . . . It is the *intent* of the action and its spirit and flavor that count.

> Joseph I. Breen
> *1936*

It is an exceedingly great comfort to us to note the outstanding success of the crusade. Because of your vigilance and because of the pressure which has been brought to bear by public opinion, the motion picture has shown improvement from the moral standpoint; crime and vice are portrayed less frequently; sin no longer is so openly approved or acclaimed; false ideals of life no longer are presented in so flagrant a manner to the impressionable minds of youth.

> Pope Pius XI in an encyclical
> letter discussing the effects of
> the Production Code
> Administration
> *1936*

It is my contention that this word as used in the picture *Gone With the Wind* is not an oath or a curse. The worst that could be said against it is that it is a vulgarism, and it is so described in the *Oxford English Dictionary*.

> David O. Selznick defending
> the "damn" in "Frankly, my
> dear, I don't give a damn"
> *1939*

"It's a helluva town" is unacceptable.

> Breen Office memorandum on
> the song "New York, New
> York" in *On the Town*
> *circa 1948*

Miscegenation (sex relationship between the white and black races) is forbidden.

> From the Production Code;
> quoted in a Breen Office
> memorandum on the remake
> of *Show Boat*
> *circa 1950*

We wish to remind you that we cannot approve photographing women in their underwear. Please bear this in mind when Don runs through the dressing room [*Singin' in the Rain*].

> Breen Office memorandum
> *circa 1951*

I want to put myself on record . . . that I may be sore as hell about what the hell is done to please the Legion, and if I'm sore as hell, nothing in this wide world will keep me silent. To quote an old Jewish proverb, if someone spits in my face, I will not say it's raining.

> Elia Kazan on the proposed
> changes in *A Streetcar Named
> Desire* to satisfy the Catholic
> Legion of Decency
> *1951*

Sanitized violence in movies has been accepted for years. What seems to upset everybody now is the showing of the consequences of violence.

> Stanley Kubrick on the
> graphic violence in *A
> Clockwork Orange*
>> *circa 1970s*

It was okay . . . to put Victor Mature in a brief tunic or to wrap him in a loincloth with his navel showing, but if Hedy [Lamarr]'s navel was exposed, it was censored. If I stuffed it with a pearl, we got by.

> Edith Head on *Samson and
> Delilah*
>> *circa 1980*

It also said in that [Breen] list that when the door opens to a bathroom, it's understood that no toilet will be visible. And the public must have thought that until 1955 or so America had no toilets.

> Joseph L. Mankiewicz
>> *circa 1980s*

When the Catholic church or its censors were about to ban some picture or insist upon having something cut out of a picture, [Louis B.] Mayer went to the court of last resort. . . . He'd pick up the phone and call the cardinal.

> Judge Lester Roth on Mayer's
> friendship with Cardinal
> Francis Spellman
>> *circa 1980s*

I believe what Jesus said, but Jesus never said priests couldn't be fools.

> Jean-Luc Godard on the
> Pope's opposition to *Hail
> Mary*
>
> *1985*

Can I do the American remake of *Hail Mary*? Divine would be great in the role.

> John Waters
>
> *1986*

If Joe Breen were alive today, I think he'd be a nervous wreck, seeing what goes on on the screen.

> Hal B. Wallis
>
> *1985*

Comedies

There are only a handful of possible jokes. The chief members of this joke band may be said to be: the fall of dignity; mistaken identity. Almost every joke on the screen belongs, roughly, to one or the other of these clans.

Mack Sennett

1918

Nearly every one of us lives in the secret hope that someday before he dies he will be able to swat a policeman's hat down around his ears. Lacking the courage and the opportunity, we like to see it done in the movies.

Mack Sennett

1918

How long a moment of pathos in a comedy may be allowed to run is like the timing of a gag. We can argue the question, work over it, and experiment in the studio, but it's the audience that gives us the answer. . . . It is like the answer to the question: "What makes 'em laugh?" We don't know.

Buster Keaton

1926

At first I did not get the glasses right; they were too big. In about the third picture I had them as I wanted them. They just fitted and did not even cover the eyebrows. I have worn them in every picture since.

Harold Lloyd

1926

[ERNST] LUBITSCH MUST MAKE MORE THRILLING PICTURE AND NOT WORRY SO MUCH ABOUT STORY. HIS PICTURES ARE OVER PEOPLE'S HEADS HERE.

Harry Warner in London to
Jack L. Warner in Hollywood
1926

I let the audience use their imagination. Can I help it if they misconstrue my suggestions?

Ernst Lubitsch on sexual
innuendo
circa 1930s

Suppose we do throw some pies, but let's throw more pies than anybody has ever thrown before. Let's throw so many pies that when we're finished, nobody will ever throw another pie again!

Stan Laurel suggesting an
epic pie fight for *The Battle of
the Century*
1927

What are they laughing about?

Margaret Dumont to Groucho
Marx
circa 1930s

Forget bus pictures.

> Harry Cohn on hearing the
> story for *It Happened One
> Night*
>> *circa 1933*

Get her out of here. I'll do it. That's not *my* leg!

> Claudette Colbert on the
> attempt to substitute a
> double's leg in the
> hitchhiking scene in *It
> Happened One Night*
>> *1933*

"We . . . have in mind we should do this as a comedy horse
opera."
"Whom do you have in mind for the horse?"

> Universal Pictures official and
> Mae West on *My Little
> Chickadee*
>> *circa 1938*

I'm afraid Bill has slipped off the wagon this morning. He's
telling the kid actors to go out and play in the traffic.

> Assistant director for *My Little
> Chickadee* on W.C. Fields's
> promise not to drink while
> making the film
>> *circa 1939*

In the past, the Lubitsch type of sophisticated light comedy
has always failed to impress mass audiences. Critics like it,
studio executives like it, our wives like it—but the cash cus-
tomers don't like it!

> Robert Lord, screenwriter and
> producer
>
> *1939*

If I appear in a bathing suit, I know it's the end of me. I
know that and I'm prepared to end my career, but it will also
be the end of the motion picture industry.

> James Stewart, refusing to
> disrobe for *The Philadelphia
> Story*
>
> *circa 1939*

Go West has again been postponed. I don't know why the
studio doesn't come right out and say they are afraid to make
it. All I get from them is a weekly announcement to come to
the wardrobe department and be fitted for a pair of early-
American pants.

> Groucho Marx
>
> *1940*

I just don't understand your attitude. Even if you plan on
rereleasing your picture [*Casablanca*], I am sure that the average movie fan could learn in time to distinguish between
Ingrid Bergman and Harpo. I don't know whether I could, but
I certainly would like to try.

> Groucho Marx arguing with
> Warner Bros. about the right
> to use the title *A Night in
> Casablanca*
>
> *circa 1945*

Who the hell is going to care about an old man who thinks he's Santa Claus?

> Darryl F. Zanuck on hearing
> the story outline for *Miracle
> on 34th Street*
> > *circa 1946*

I've told you a thousand times there's too goddamned much mush in this thing!

> Walt Disney objecting to a
> kissing scene in *The Absent-
> Minded Professor*
> > *circa 1960*

I hate to admit this, but Doris [Day] is a tall, well-built girl, and I just couldn't tote her around for as long and as far as required; so they built a special shelf for me with two hooks on it and she sat on the shelf, and all I did was hold her legs and shoulders.

> Rock Hudson on carrying
> Doris Day through the streets
> in *Pillow Talk*
> > *circa 1960s*

I started work on the screenplay [of *Dr. Strangelove*] with every intention of making the film a serious treatment.... [I]deas kept coming to me which I would discard because they were so ludicrous. I kept saying to myself: "I can't do this. People will laugh." But after a month or so I began to realize that all the things I was throwing out were the things which were most truthful.

Stanley Kubrick
circa 1960s

You don't live and work with a guy as long as I did without the divorce being painful.

Jerry Lewis on breaking up
with Dean Martin
circa 1960s

The whole character is one moment out of my life, me at twenty-one years old in a drugstore trying to ask for prophylactics, sweating, and walking out as soon as the druggist's wife started to wait on me.

Dustin Hoffman on Benjamin
Braddock in *The Graduate*
1968

I remember sitting with Ralph [Rosenblum] in the cutting room at five o'clock preparing for a seven o'clock screening that night and saying, "Let's go down to the sound studio and I'll put a jump at the end of the picture [*Annie Hall*] and wing the joke about the eggs." At five-thirty that night we got into the recording booth, ran back uptown, and stuck that joke in, and it stayed forever.

Woody Allen
circa 1970s

Babe [Oliver Hardy] would do anything Stan [Laurel] suggested. To him he was a god, and he had the greatest respect for Stan's genius for thinking up comic situations.

> Billy Gilbert, comedian who
> worked with the team
> *circa 1970s*

He really is a funny, funny fellow, isn't he?

> Stan Laurel on Oliver Hardy
> *circa 1930s*

Well, it was pretty sad for Cary Grant going around on his hands and knees looking for a bone.

> Howard Hawks on the gloomy
> lighting in *Bringing Up Baby*
> *circa 1970s*

[Rosalind Russell] told [Howard] Hawks she didn't want me to have any bullets; she thought I was a little off. "He's liable to shoot me," she said.

> John Qualen on playing the
> convicted killer Earl Williams
> in *His Girl Friday*
> *circa 1970s*

"Ryan, we're in a piece of shit! I mean, we're *really* in trouble. . . . *I* know what's funny and *this isn't funny!*"
"Well, I kinda—sorta—think it's funny."

> Barbra Streisand and Ryan
> O'Neal on the set of *What's
> Up, Doc?*
> *circa 1971*

So what if some people were annoyed with the love story [in *A Night at the Opera*]? . . . [Irving] Thalberg was smarter. He knew not everybody was crazy about comedy.

> Groucho Marx
> *circa 1973*

"Groucho, I must tell you—I've seen *A Night at the Opera* seventeen times."
"Really?"
"Yes. I just couldn't get over that love story between Allan Jones and Kitty Carlisle!"

> Mike Nichols and Groucho Marx
> *circa 1960s*

I approached Cary [Grant] to do the role of the paleontologist [in *Bringing Up Baby*]. . . . [Grant said,] "I wouldn't know how to tackle it. I'm not an intellectual type." And I said, "You've seen Harold Lloyd, haven't you?" He nodded. That gave him a clue—the innocent abroad.

> Howard Hawks
> *circa 1975*

What really concerns people are the motivations and the subtleties of psychological anxiety and neurosis, and these are not subjects for the traditional cinematic comedian.

> Woody Allen
> *1977*

Very little of the film [*Annie Hall*] is autobiographical. . . . I was not born underneath a roller coaster on Coney Island, nor was my first wife politically active, nor was my second wife a member of the literary set, nor did Diane [Keaton] leave me for a rock star or to live in California.

Woody Allen

circa 1980

I didn't have to worry about authenticity [in Paramount's *Road* movies]. If somebody wrote and said, "Edith, in Morocco they don't wear headdresses like that," I didn't give a damn. If Bob Hope wanted to wear it because it was funny, he wore it.

Edith Head

circa 1980

I always had the idea of *Diner* in my head. But it never made sense to me—what we did in those days and why. Then one day it occurred to me: It was that we really didn't know how to communicate with girls. By upbringing, boys play with boys. . . . Then, at some point, you're supposed to get married and not run back to the boys. But where's the preparation for spending your whole life with a woman?

Barry Levinson

1982

That would have been a good idea. I guess he'd live in the ghetto and probably be a mild-mannered sanitation engineer.

Richard Pryor on the
suggestion that he should
have played a black Superman
in *Superman III*

1983

Directing this movie [*Beverly Hills Cop*] was like doing live television. . . . We were reshaping the material every day, and whenever we needed inspiration, Eddie [Murphy] would provide it.

Martin Brest

1985

The only thing I'm secure about is that I'm funny.

Eddie Murphy

1982

Critics and Awards

Forget it. You ain't got a Chinaman's chance. They only vote for that arty junk.

> Harry Cohn to Frank Capra on his chances for an Academy Award for *American Madness*
> *circa 1932*

What a wonderful thing—this benefit for David Selznick.

> Bob Hope on the Academy Awards ceremony the year of *Gone With the Wind*
> *1940*

Don't make the best picture you ever made in the year that someone makes *Gone With the Wind*.

> Frank Capra on the lack of Academy Awards for *Mr. Smith Goes to Washington*
> *1971*

One can't cash it.

> David O. Selznick on the
> value of a good review
>
> *1957*

Okay, Charlie [Chaplin] doesn't make us laugh anymore. On the other hand, his critics make me laugh.

> François Truffaut
>
> *1957*

I lost to a tracheotomy!

> Shirley MacLaine on losing
> the 1961 Academy Award to
> Elizabeth Taylor, winner of
> what was considered a
> sympathy award for her
> operation
>
> *circa 1960*

I have the personality of a successful actor, which encourages critics all over the world to think it's about time they took me down a peg or two; you know: "It would do him some good to tell him that he's not all that great." But they've been telling me that for twenty-five years!

> Orson Welles
>
> *circa 1960s*

In Europe they're just as snobbish as they are in New York. They like foreign pictures.

> William Wyler
>
> *circa 1960s*

You may have noticed . . . that when I get jumped on for a
bad movie, you never hear a peep out of me. You never hear
any refutations, no placing the blame somewhere else. . . .
The next time around, if it's a great success, you still won't
hear one damn peep out of me. That's the way I live.

Sidney Poitier
circa 1971

My first reaction of these guys is, "Who cares?"

Jack Nicholson on critics
circa 1975

It's sort of a popularity test. When it's your turn, you win it.

Woody Allen on the Academy
Awards
1979

I never thought about that until I kept seeing it mentioned
in the reviews.

Harrison Ford on comparisons
between his style of acting
and John Wayne's
circa 1984

You know what my Oscar for Emma Goldman [in *Reds*] got
me? I got fewer offers for less money.

Maureen Stapleton
1984

Getting an Oscar for *The Philadelphia Story* was the easiest Oscar that you could imagine. All I had to do was get out of the way.

> Donald Ogden Stewart on
> adapting Philip Barry's play
> for the movies
> *circa 1985*

I'm not one of those actors who will send the cleaning lady up to accept the award in my place.

> Sean Connery
> *1988*

Directors

Let Jack Ford direct it. He yells good.

> Carl Laemmle, studio head,
> Universal Pictures
>
> *1919*

I never want anything shown to me as a design that you could possibly buy or wear. I want something original.

> Cecil B. De Mille to costume
> designer Edith Head
>
> *circa 1920s*

I have not much patience with a thing of beauty that must be explained to be understood. If it does need added interpretation by someone other than the creator, then I question whether it has fulfilled its purpose.

> Charles Chaplin
>
> *1924*

Anybody can invent plots, which is only crossing and criss-crossing. I think I hate plots.

> Charles Chaplin
>
> *1924*

[A] picture must be *pictorial*. There must be something to photograph every minute. Something must take place every second. Action—and I do not necessarily mean spectacular or violent action—should be the essence of the screen tale.

Allan Dwan

1926

The movie and the radio will bring people together. They will make for unity and for a certain great oneness in the world. Ultimately it may even be oneness with God.

Cecil B. De Mille

1927

They say that I have a passion for "camera angles." But I do not take trick scenes from unusual positions just to get startling effects. To me the camera represents the eye of a person, through whose mind one is watching the events on the screen. It must follow characters at times into difficult places. . . . It must whirl and peep and move from place to place as swiftly as thought itself. . . . I think the films of the future will use more and more of these "camera angles," or, as I prefer to call them, these "dramatic angles." They help to photograph thought.

F. W. Murnau

1928

I . . . FEEL THAT WE MUST DISMISS [JACK] FORD AS A MAN WHO IS NO MORE SUREFIRE THAN IS [GEORGE] CUKOR. BOTH ARE GREAT DIRECTORS AND BOTH HAVE TO HAVE THEIR STORIES SELECTED FOR THEM AND GUIDED FOR THEM, AND PRESUMABLY FORD NEEDS THE SAME GUIDANCE IN SCRIPT THAT CUKOR DOES.

David O. Selznick

1937

I am somewhat wounded, since this is the first time in my career that anyone has said that he did not want to work for me, but I don't suppose there is anything I can do except bandage up the wound.

> David O. Selznick on John
> Ford's refusal to work for him
> *1937*

Do you think [director William] Wyler is mad at Henry Fonda or something because of their past? It seems that he is not content to okay anything with Fonda until it has been done ten or eleven takes. After all, they have been divorced from the same girl [Margaret Sullavan]. . . . Possibly Wyler likes to see these big numbers on the slate, and maybe we could arrange to have them start with number six on each take, then it wouldn't take so long to get up to nine or ten.

> Hal B. Wallis to supervisor
> Henry Blanke on *Jezebel*
> *1937*

In my case, directorial style must be largely the absence of style. . . . [I am] best pleased when the finished picture shows to the layman in the audience no visible sign of "direction," but merely seems to be a smooth and convincing presentation by the players of the subject in hand.

> George Cukor
> *1938*

I'm not interested in logic; I'm interested in effect. If the audience ever thinks about logic, it's on their way home after the show, and by that time, you see, they've paid for their tickets.

> Alfred Hitchcock
> *circa 1940*

I try to make people forget they're in a theater. I don't want them to be conscious of a camera or a screen. I want them to feel that what they're seeing is real.

John Ford
circa 1940s

"Howard, how can any man in his right mind make two or three reels of a picture about a man shooting a gun?"
"I don't know, Ernst. How the hell can a man in his right mind make two or three reels of people coming in and out of doorways?"

Ernst Lubitsch and
Howard Hawks
circa 1940s

Actors! Actors! They want to know everything!

Michael Curtiz, approached
for information by his actors
on the set of *Casablanca*
1943

When the last dime is gone, I'll go sit on the curb outside with a pencil and a ten-cent notebook and start the whole thing over again.

Preston Sturges, when facing
bankruptcy
circa 1950

I hate pictures. . . . Well, I like *making* them, of course. . . . But it's no use asking me to talk about art.

John Ford

circa 1950s

I recall being on a streetcar many years ago with him [John Ford] at night. We sat facing a compartment window at the middle of the car and suddenly I noticed Ford was staring at this glass with deep interest. He was seeing a double reflection . . . and at the same time looking through at people in the front section of the car. . . . I could see him making a mental note to try to catch that with a camera at the next opportunity.

Dudley Nichols, screenwriter
1953

When one is born and reared in the home of a minister, one has a chance at an early age to catch a glimpse behind the scenes of life and death. . . . The devil became an early acquaintance, and, in the way of a child, it was necessary to render him concrete.

Ingmar Bergman on his childhood
1954

It genuinely seemed to strike them as a radical suggestion, as though I'd asked to have my mother direct the picture.

Charlton Heston on his suggestion to Universal officials that Orson Welles direct *Touch of Evil*
1957

You have some strange phobia against short scenes.

> David O. Selznick to John
> Huston during the making of
> *A Farewell to Arms*
>
> *1957*

I want to climb up there and change everything. It's like meeting a girl you slept with fifteen years ago. You look at her and you think, "My God, did I go to bed with that?"

> Alfred Hitchcock on his
> old films
>
> *circa 1960s*

Perhaps I have become a "big film" man.

> David Lean after *Lawrence
> of Arabia*
>
> *circa 1960s*

As you mull it over, you begin to see a form, a style. . . . You can't see a single detail, you don't know how to put it all together, but that doesn't matter. You can see this form, this style. I think it is largely a matter of intuition. I think with my stomach more than with my head.

> Vincente Minnelli on
> beginning a new film
>
> *circa 1960s*

The only film that I wrote from beginning to end and was able to complete properly was *Citizen Kane,* and too many years have gone by since I was given the chance. Can I afford to wait another fifteen years for someone who's willing to have total confidence in me again?

> Orson Welles
>
> *circa 1960s*

For me, the real tragedy of [Orson] Welles is that for thirty years he spent so much time with all-powerful producers who offered him cigars but wouldn't have given him a hundred feet of celluloid to expose.

François Truffaut

circa 1972

The director must always have the last word on the set, and I don't like any kind of discussions or arguments. . . . [I]f you have something to say, you always arrange it so nobody else need know. You take a five-minute break and they presume you are going to powder your nose, and you get the director away and discuss something. But to make a scene in front of the rest of the cast and crew would be just like mutiny.

Gloria Swanson

1964

I have a theory about the public: If the Elizabethan public were not one of genius, Mr. Marlowe and Mr. Shakespeare would have stopped after two plays. . . . The collaboration with the public is important—with them you can do something, without them you cannot—the cinema is too expensive.

René Clair

circa 1969

Anybody who says that every picture is not a collaboration is an idiot. It's a question of how much you collaborate and who you collaborate with.

Stanley Donen

circa 1969

DIRECTORS

What survives best is myth, poetry. Realism dies.

> Rouben Mamoulian
> *circa 1969*

George [Lucas] directs like John Ford. He doesn't really work a lot with his actors or tell them a lot. But he constructs his scenes so specifically, or narrowly—like a railroad track—that everything comes out more or less the way he sees it.

> Francis Ford Coppola
> *circa 1970s*

All I'm doing is telling a story.

> Howard Hawks
> *circa 1970s*

I learned right in the beginning from Jack [John] Ford, and I learned what not to do by watching Cecil De Mille.

> Howard Hawks
> *circa 1970s*

[John] Ford and I said, "They talk too much," and we cut down the dialogue on every scene we made. We cut lines out because actors just loved it when they got a whole bunch of lines.

> Howard Hawks on the
> transition to sound movies
> *circa 1970s*

They've gone through their growth period, indulging their esoteric tastes. Coppola isn't interested any more in filming a pomegranate growing in the desert. They're all very commercial now.

> Frank Yablans on the young
> generation of filmmakers
> *circa 1970s*

I think [Alfred] Hitchcock was the only director who was independent of [David O.] Selznick. . . . On any of Hitchcock's pictures, if a producer or author came onto the set, he'd stop the camera and say there was a mechanical fault. Soon they got the hint that the camera would work when they were *not* present, but not while they were on the set.

> Ingrid Bergman
> *1972*

[Howard Hawks] wouldn't allow [producer Howard] Hughes on the set. From there on, even at Warners, I think he got away with it. And that's pretty tough to do when you're talking about Jack Warner. But he couldn't get away with it at MGM.

> John Lee Mahin on why
> Hawks didn't work much for
> MGM
> *1979*

[Sergio Leone] had found a cinematic trick: BIG close-ups. He would say to me . . . "You begin CLOSE-UP! Two beeg green eyes!" Of course, that's how Clint Eastwood became a star.

> Peter Bogdanovich
> *1973*

When you're directing children, you have to treat them as if they're forty.

> Peter Bogdanovich on
> directing Tatum O'Neal and
> P. J. Johnson in *Paper Moon*
> *1973*

I don't say, "Now I'm going to tell you a moral tale and you'd better like it." No, first I entertain them. I get them in a spirit of laughter and then, perhaps, they might be softened up to accept some kind of moral precept.

> Frank Capra
> *circa 1975*

I would prefer to write all this down, however tiny and however short the pieces of film are—they should be written down in just the same way a composer writes down those little black dots from which we get beautiful sound. So I usually start with the writer long before dialogue comes into it, and I get on paper a description of what comes on that screen. It's as though you ran a film on the screen and turned off all the sound so you would see the images filling the screen one after the other.

> Alfred Hitchcock
> *circa 1975*

If I were to make a film about the life of a *sole,* it would end up being about me.

> Federico Fellini
> *circa 1976*

Movies now have gone past the phase of prose narrative and are coming nearer and nearer to poetry. I am trying to free my work from certain constrictions—a story with a beginning, a development, an ending. It should be more like a poem, with meter and cadence.

> Federico Fellini
> *circa 1976*

Of course I call myself an artist. What should I call myself —a plumber?

> Federico Fellini
> *circa 1976*

Picture-makers lead dozens of lives—a life for each picture. And, by the same token, they perish a little when each picture is finished and that world comes to an end. In this respect, it is a melancholy occupation.

> John Huston
> *circa 1976*

Now act more like a princess. Stand up straight.

> George Lucas to Carrie Fisher
> on the set of *Star Wars*
> *circa 1976*

The problem with [Alfred] Hitchcock is that he's wonderful to work with on a screenplay—he's inventive; he's cautious; he's charming; he's everything. He's also a very cold man, a vain man, I believe. I don't really think he likes people. I think that's why he enjoys killing them in suspense pictures.

> John Michael Hayes, screenwriter
> *circa 1978*

I found it laboriously irritating to direct. I have absolutely no powers of command. If I asked somebody to do something and they'd say, "What did you say?"—I'd say, "Well, don't do it. Don't do it if you don't feel like it. I just thought you should walk over there." And they'd say, "Hey, c'mon . . . why should I walk over there?"

> Walter Matthau
>
> *1978*

You cannot overemphasize the importance he has had. If this generation is to change American cinema, he is to be given the credit, or the discredit. Whichever it may be.

> John Milius on Francis Ford Coppola
>
> *circa 1978*

I just wanted to be an ordinary parish priest.

> Martin Scorsese on his early ambitions.
>
> *circa 1978*

I've discovered I've got this preoccupation with ordinary people pursued by large forces.

> Steven Spielberg
>
> *circa 1978*

I think it's all about Bernardo Bertolucci's psychoanalysis. . . . *He* didn't know what it was about either.

> Marlon Brando on *Last Tango in Paris*
>
> *circa 1979*

The crew working on the film [*Apocalypse Now*] were not following some cohesive idea that they knew or some logical script; they were following some madman's. . . . I didn't have the heart to tell them I didn't know what I was doing.

Francis Ford Coppola

1979

Because that's how I remember it when I was small.

Woody Allen on why
Manhattan was filmed in
black and white

circa 1980

You have more respect for a bad film from Fritz Lang than for a good film from Hal Ashby—if there were any good films from Hal Ashby, which there are not.

Jean-Luc Godard

1980

Making movies is a bit like having babies. It lasts nine months, and you go through morning sickness.

Guy Hamilton, director of
James Bond films

1980

We have a violent society. It's not Greece; it's not Athens; it's not the Renaissance—it's the American society, and I would have to personify it by saying that it is a violent one. So why not make films about it?

Arthur Penn, director of
Bonnie and Clyde

circa 1980s

I want to make *The Grace Metalious Story*. She wrote *Peyton Place*, became rich, bought Cadillacs, and killed herself. That's a great American story.

John Waters

1981

I got a call from Mr. [Joseph] Schenck to come up to the Loew's building, overlooking Times Square. He said, "My boy, look down there at the theater—it's eleven o'clock in the morning, it's raining, and people are standing in line to see your movie. Why are they standing in line? Why do they like this movie?" I said, "I don't know—I don't know why they stay away; I don't know why they go in." He said, "You won't tell me. But, you know, it shows that you *know something*—because they're buying tickets."

Richard Brooks on *The Blackboard Jungle*

1982

If [John] Huston really likes a property, there's no person who can put it on the screen better. But if he is not entirely sold on the thing he is doing, he can make a bomb.

W. R. Burnett, screenwriter
circa 1982

Preston Sturges was one of the best, but crazy, a little nutty. He had a big desk and a horn on it that honked. Honk, honk. He thought it was goddamned funny.

W. R. Burnett, screenwriter
circa 1982

[Michael] Curtiz needed somebody to sit on him. He didn't have any judgment about what to make.

> W. R. Burnett, screenwriter
> *circa 1982*

Take "myself," subtract "movies," and the result is "zero."

> Akira Kurosawa
> *1982*

No matter how much difficulty you had in obtaining a particular shot, the audience will never know. If it is not interesting, it simply isn't interesting.

> Akira Kurosawa
> *1982*

I'll not bullshit any of you about the symbolism I intended. If I intended it, I'll tell you.

> Steven Spielberg
> *1982*

That was sort of my '41-gate.

> Steven Spielberg on the box-office flop *1941*
> *1982*

Well, we waited for the sun to get very low, then we told the kids to go fly their bicycles across the sun. We said, "Ride like the wind; ride like the wind." And, wow—they flew right across. . . .

> Steven Spielberg explaining the special effects in *E.T.*
> *1982*

When you are writing, you are alone and can confine your foolishness to a room, but when you work with people, when you're directing, it's quite possible to feel like the biggest idiot on earth.

Robert Towne

circa 1982

Writing is creating something out of nothing. [Directing] is creating something out of what is there—but doing it with fifty-five thousand people and trucks and equipment standing around staring at you, wondering what you are going to do next, or if you know what the hell you're doing.

Robert Towne

circa 1982

I remember the moment I was first told about the existence of the auteur theory. I listened and listened as the explanation went on, and all I could think was this: "What's the punch line?"

William Goldman,
screenwriter

1983

What is directing? It's trying to use a lot of people and some very, very heavy apparatus and give it the lightness of a pen while you are writing.

David Lean

circa 1983

I took one look at the amount of work and thought, Oh, my God, my life is complicated enough.

> George Lucas on why he
> didn't direct *Return of the
> Jedi*
>
> *1983*

He has an idea about every thirteen seconds.

> Frank J. Marshall, Jr.,
> producer, on Steven Spielberg
> *circa 1983*

The most important thing about directing [is] to be in good physical shape.

> Sidney Pollack
>
> *circa 1983*

He's more John Ford; I'm more Hitchcock.

> François Truffaut on Steven
> Spielberg
> *circa 1983*

I remember asking Warren Beatty if I could rehearse a scene [from *Reds*] just a little. So we rehearsed after work at night, and we rehearsed Saturday, and we rehearsed Sunday, and that was the *last* time I opened my mouth to Warren.

> Maureen Stapleton
>
> *1984*

[Hitchcock was] literate to the extent of reading. . . . [B]ut I must admit his form of reading was he liked to read the dirtiest parts of *Ulysses* and things like that.

Charles Bennett, screenwriter
circa 1985

Mr. Hitchcock did not say actors are cattle. He said they should be treated like cattle.

James Stewart
1985

[Victor] Fleming was a formidable character, a big, full-blooded romantic man, who liked working with the big male stars of Hollywood because they acted out his own fantasies for him.

Michael Powell
circa 1986

John [Huston] managed within the last years to summon up yet more energy, more purpose, to make damn sure his children were on their feet and thriving. Having done that, he made a beautiful picture, *The Dead.* . . . And having done that, he said farewell to all that.

Peter O'Toole
1987

George Romero basically made *Night of the Living Dead* his first time out of the gate. That's a little like Orson Welles making *Citizen Kane*, strictly in the sense that when your first film goes out and becomes what that became, that's a tough act to follow.

> Richard Rubinstein, George
> A. Romero associate
> *circa 1987*

I remember being at a point below his knees and looking up at the vast length of him. He was six foot three; his voice was big. He was devastatingly attractive—even to his daughter as a child. . . . [H]is voice was so beautiful, so enveloping. He was just bigger and better than anyone else.

> Anjelica Huston on her father,
> John Huston
> *circa 1989*

Drama and Adventure

It will be a tough job to get a satisfactory picture out of this material, but I believe it can be done.

> Wally Kline, screenwriter, on
> *Everybody Comes to Rick's,*
> which became *Casablanca*
> 1942

[Ilsa] tells Rick that she loves him and will do anything he wants. She will go anywhere, stay here, anything. She is absolutely helpless in the great passionate love she has for him. . . . She knows she is being wicked, but she can't help herself. This is a great scene for a woman to play.

> Casey Robinson, screenwriter,
> offering suggestions on
> *Casablanca*
> 1942

All characters in "B" pictures are too smart.

> Joe Sistrom, Paramount
> producer
> *circa 1944*

I want you to write it in your own way—the story you have to tell from your own knowledge.

> Samuel Goldwyn to
> MacKinlay Kantor, Air Force
> correspondent, on the story
> that became *The Best Years of
> Our Lives*
> *1944*

Bob, listen, you said to yourself, "Now I'm in Hollywood, writing a Hollywood picture." . . . But I don't want you to think of this as a Hollywood picture. I want something simple and believable.

> Samuel Goldwyn to Robert E.
> Sherwood, on the screenplay
> of *The Best Years of Our Lives*
> *1946*

Frank, if you want to do a movie about me committing suicide and an angel that hasn't won its wings named Clarence, I'm your boy. Anything, Frank. Anything.

> James Stewart to Frank Capra,
> when presented with the plot
> of *It's a Wonderful Life*
> *1945*

I thought it was the greatest film I had ever made. Better yet, I thought it was the greatest film *anybody* ever made.

> Frank Capra on *It's a
> Wonderful Life*
> *1971*

"Katie—setting off with John in a little plane—how can you —*how?* You may be killed. Then what . . . ?"

"Well, John may be killed."

"The hell with John. I can't control John, you know that. But you—I'm photographing you. You're a reasonable, decent human being."

> Sam Spiegel and Katharine Hepburn, on elephant hunting with John Huston during the filming of *The African Queen*
> *1950*

Your interpretation of Rosie is doing harm to the picture as well as hurting the character. Did you ever see Mrs. Roosevelt visiting the soldiers in the hospitals in the newsreels? Well, I think of [Rosie] a little bit as Mrs. Roosevelt.

> John Huston to Katharine Hepburn, on her character in *The African Queen*
> *circa 1950*

Did they stay in Africa? I always thought they must have. And lots of little Charlies and Rosies. And lived happily ever after.

> Katharine Hepburn on the main characters in *The African Queen*
> *circa 1987*

[The first script for *The Bridge on the River Kwai*] was rubbish—filled with elephant charges and that sort of thing. . . . I found Colonel Nicholson to be a blinkered character. . . . Then Sam Spiegel . . . took me to dinner. He is a very persuasive character. I started out maintaining that I wouldn't play the role, and by the end of the evening we were discussing what kind of wig I should wear.

> Alec Guinness on *The Bridge on the River Kwai*
> *circa 1950s*

You'll have to get a director who understands the colonel—I don't.

> John Ford to Sam Spiegel, turning down *The Bridge on the River Kwai*
> *circa 1956*

One day I killed 681.

> Alec Guinness on killing flies during the filming of *The Bridge on the River Kwai*
> *circa 1950s*

Everybody knows Lincoln was a great man, but the idea of the picture [*Young Mr. Lincoln*] was to give the feeling that even as a young man you could sense there was going to be something great about this man.

> John Ford
> *circa 1960s*

What the fuck is all this shit about you not wanting to play this picture? You think Lincoln's a great fucking Emancipator, huh? He's a young jack-legged lawyer from Springfield, for Christ sake.

> John Ford convincing Henry Fonda to take the lead in *Young Mr. Lincoln*
> *circa 1938*

Suddenly Last Summer is really just a fancy story of Mother Love.

> Sam Marx, MGM story editor
> *circa 1950s*

Sure, he's a snooper, but aren't we all?

> Alfred Hitchcock on the hero
> of *Rear Window*
> *1962*

I didn't want to wind up with a completely happy ending [for *To Catch a Thief*]. That's why I put in that scene by the tree, when Cary Grant agrees to marry Grace Kelly. It turns out that the mother-in-law will come and live with them, so the final note is pretty grim.

> Alfred Hitchcock
> *1962*

The film was a costume designer's dream.

> Edith Head on *To Catch a Thief*
> *circa 1980*

Our original title, you know, was *The Man in Lincoln's Nose*. Couldn't use it, though. They also wouldn't let us shoot people on Mount Rushmore. Can't deface a national monument. And it's a pity, too, because I had a wonderful shot in mind of Cary Grant hiding in Lincoln's nose and having a sneezing fit.

> Alfred Hitchcock on *North by Northwest*
> *circa 1960s*

Whenever I've tangled with a beautiful spy, have you noticed what invariably happens? Even if I know the girl is a nasty and dangerous little snake, I've still had to kiss her first and kill her later.

Sean Connery
1964

[Richard] Burton has a magnificent voice. Let him do the talking, I'll do the killing.

Clint Eastwood to Brian G.
Hutton, director of *Where
Eagles Dare*
circa 1968

Simple themes save us from the nuances.

John Wayne on *The Green
Berets*
circa 1968

We made a picture that worked pretty well called *The Big
Sleep,* and I never figured out what was going on, but I thought that the basic thing had great scenes in it and it was good entertainment. After that got by, I said, "I'm never going to worry about being logical again."

Howard Hawks
circa 1970s

Johnny Huston did such a good script for me [on *Sergeant York*] that I suggested to [Jack L.] Warner that they make him a director. Johnny came back and said, "What should I write?" And I said, "Don't write anything. It's hard enough to direct your first picture. There's a story that Warners owns that I've always been going to do called *The Maltese Falcon. . . .*" And he and I were up against each other for an Academy Award at the end of the year.

Howard Hawks
circa 1970s

They had me cowdogging and saying, "Yes, ma'am" and "No, ma'am" all the damn time. I was beginning to wonder if they ever were going to let me show some balls! I brought this up with Pappy [John Ford] and he just gave me a dirty look. But later he changed the scene and said, "Duke, I'm going to let you do what you always do when a broad locks you out. I'm going to let you kick the fuckin' door down."

John Wayne on *The Quiet Man*
circa 1970s

Maybe a lot of people just don't want to see Clint Eastwood's leg cut off.

Jennings Lang on why *The Beguiled* failed at the box office
circa 1971

Francis [Ford Coppola] had a book in his hand, and it was *The Godfather.* He told me, "I was at Paramount all day yesterday, and they want me to direct this hunk of trash. I don't want to do it. I want to do art films. . . ." I told him to make the film, make some money, and then he could do what he wanted to do.

> Carmine Coppola
> *circa 1984*

In a way the Mafia is the best example of capitalists we have. Don Corleone is just any ordinary American business magnate who is trying to do the best he can for the group he represents and for his family.

> Marlon Brando on his role in
> *The Godfather*
> *circa 1972*

This time I really set out to destroy the family. Yet I wanted to destroy it in the way that I think is most profound—from the inside.

> Francis Ford Coppola on *The Godfather, Part II*
> *circa 1974*

In New York City, if you drive like that, they don't pay too much attention.

> William Friedkin on filming the chase scene in *The French Connection*
> *1974*

His [Hal B. Wallis's] first question was, "What's it about?" I said, "It's about a woman who dies of cancer of the brain." Well, the man turned white, of course. . . . One must remem-

ber that this is the mid-thirties and that cancer was a dirty
word.

> Casey Robinson on his idea
> for adapting a play called
> *Dark Victory*
>
> *1974*

Jack's the only actor who could wear it for three quarters of
a movie and get away with it.

> Robert Evans on the bandage
> on Jack Nicholson's nose in
> *Chinatown*
>
> *circa 1975*

I'm glad it had a down ending. It's remembered, and that's
the greatest wealth in the world—to be remembered.

> Robert Evans on *Chinatown*
> *circa 1980s*

There was no part for me [in *The Taking of Pelham One
Two Three*], except the black Transit Authority patrolman—
who was about thirty-two. I said, "Well, I'm a little older than
thirty-two, but I think there's a lot of black in my background
—although I'm not sure." . . . So they gave me the part.

> Walter Matthau
> *1978*

My film is not about Vietnam. It *is* Vietnam. It's what it was
really like.

> Francis Ford Coppola on
> *Apocalypse Now*
>
> *1979*

I wanted the audience to feel another dimension in her. She's the forgotten person in the screenplay and also in the other characters' lives.

Meryl Streep on her character
in *The Deer Hunter*
1979

One of the rules with the Bond pictures is that you're not allowed to have a leading lady who can act—because we can't afford them. . . . [I]f ever we were to have a real leading lady, the next time around we'd have to have another one. And in no time at all we'd have to have Jane Fonda for $2 million and up.

Guy Hamilton, director of
several Bond films
1980

You know why I did that kind of lighting we used? Because it was quicker and cheaper. . . . You light the person, you throw a shadow across the back wall, and you're lit. . . . The French, who don't accept anything until they've pigeonholed it, had to call it *film noir* because they couldn't understand it.

Edward Dmytryk on *film noir*
circa 1980s

I was at his [Alan Ladd's] house, and he took me up to the second floor, where he had a wardrobe. . . . He opened it up, and there must have been hundreds of suits, sport jackets, slacks, and shoes. He looked at me and said, "Not bad for an Okie kid, eh?" I got goose pimples, because I remembered when Gatsby took Daisy to show her his mansion. . . . I said to Sue [Carol] and Alan, "How about we do *The Great Gatsby* ... ?" ... [T]hey were a little dubious, but I talked them into it.

> Richard Maibaum,
> screenwriter
> *circa 1980s*

That casting! It's an Italian picture, and not an Italian in it. Stanley Fields, William Collier, Jr., Doug Fairbanks, Jr.— isn't that ridiculous? It drove me crazy!

> W. R. Burnett on the movie
> based on his novel *Little
> Caesar*
> *circa 1982*

The typhoid is particularly unpleasant because you go dizzy and can't stand up. But apart from that, it was a big laugh.

> Michael Caine on filming *The
> Man Who Would Be King*
> while sick with typhoid in
> Morocco
> *1983*

The public was being given the great privilege of embracing Cary Grant and Ingrid Bergman together. It was a kind of temporary ménage à trois.

> Alfred Hitchcock explaining
> the kiss over the telephone in
> *Notorious*
> *1967*

How many young men get to live with Bedouins for a year?

> Peter O'Toole on making
> *Lawrence of Arabia*
> *1983*

What kept us going was the thought that [David] Lean, at fifty-four, had done this every day for a year. David Lean was our criterion for survival.

> Steven Spielberg on filming
> *Raiders of the Lost Ark* in
> Tunisia
> *circa 1983*

I just thought this was a clever way of getting out of Tunisia early—I had no idea what the reaction would be.

> Steven Spielberg on why the
> fight between Indiana Jones
> and a scimitar swordsman
> ended with an abrupt gunshot
> in *Raiders of the Lost Ark*
> *1982*

When I lost *Raiders* . . . I thought, Well, that was my shot. From now, I'm a TV actor. I felt entitled to get something out of it and kept telling people, "That was *my* part, you know."

> Tom Selleck, considered for
> the lead in *Raiders of the Lost
> Ark*
> *circa 1983*

It's a film about character, not about war and wanting to kill.

> Tom Cruise on *Top Gun*
> *1986*

There are always people who jump with a towel from the roof because they think they are Superman.

> Robert De Niro on whether
> his role in *Taxi Driver*
> inspired real-life imitators
> *1987*

Movies don't kill people. People kill people.

> Martin Scorsese on *Taxi
> Driver* and John Hinckley, Jr.
> *1987*

Egos

What are you, the Pope or something?

> Harry Cohn to rebellious
> director Frank Capra
> *circa 1937*

There, but for the grace of God, goes God.

> Herman J. Mankiewicz on
> Orson Welles
> *circa 1940s*

Orson looked over the credits for the picture. "Orson Welles, in *Citizen Kane*. Produced by Orson Welles. Directed by Orson Welles. Screenplay by Herman J. Mankiewicz and Orson Welles." . . . And there was something in that list that seemed wrong to Orson. . . . He actually offered Herman $10,000 if he'd take his name off the picture.

> Nunnally Johnson,
> screenwriter
> *circa 1971*

My mother brought me up to be a genius, and she was one of the most successful women I've ever known.

Preston Sturges

circa 1940s

Yesterday we had considerable upset with Miss [Marlene] Dietrich in the trying on of her wardrobe. I find that after Mr. [Hal B.] Wallis okayed a change for her, when the time comes to shoot the scene she refuses to wear the wardrobe. . . . Miss Dietrich has an idea that she is to be dressed like a clothes-horse stepping out of a page of *Vogue,* rather than the wife of a lineman who makes $200 a month.

Frank Mattison, unit manager
on the set of *Manpower*

1941

I strongly feel that *The Maltese Falcon,* which you want me to do, is not an important picture and, in this connection, I must remind you again, before I signed the new contract with you, you promised me that you would not require me to perform in anything but important pictures.

George Raft to Jack L. Warner

1941

This is a movie, chowderhead, not a lifeboat.

Spencer Tracy to Garson
Kanin on why he received top
billing over Katharine
Hepburn in *Woman of the
Year*

circa 1942

Here you're working with these great talents. And what am I doing? Still playing the shop girl on the corner.

> Judy Garland to then-husband
> Vincente Minnelli
> *circa 1949*

All actors get preoccupied with billing order, but I've learned it doesn't matter a damn as long as your name's in the same size type.

> Charlton Heston
> *1957*

I have the greatest respect in the world for [Ernest] Hemingway . . . but my ego—and also my record—doesn't permit me to think that Hemingway can prepare a better motion picture than I can.

> David O. Selznick defending
> the script of *A Farewell to
> Arms*
> *1957*

You make a star, you make a monster.

> Sam Spiegel, who cast the
> unknown Peter O'Toole as
> *Lawrence of Arabia*
> *circa 1960s*

This is the biggest desk because I'm the biggest shot.

> Francis Ford Coppola
> *circa 1970s*

The reason why stars are good, they walk in through a door
and they think, Everybody wants to lay me.

> Howard Hawks
>
> *circa 1970s*

Mr. Deeds [Goes to Town] was the first film in which I
achieved filmdom's highest status—I had forced [Harry]
Cohn to feature my name above the title.

> Frank Capra
>
> *1971*

The only reason he [Dustin Hoffman] took this part was
because he was afraid Al Pacino would grab it first, and everyone knows how Dusty feels about Al.

> Film crew electrician during
> the filming of *Kramer vs.*
> *Kramer*
>
> *circa 1978*

Directors never give special mention to their editors when
they lope up to receive their Oscar—lest an overeager critic
surmise that the film had been in trouble and was saved by
heavy editorial doctoring. And editors, understanding the ex-
plosive ego issues involved, wisely stay true to the bent for
anonymity that led them to their chosen profession.

> Ralph Rosenblum, film editor
> *circa 1979*

Steve [Spielberg] seems to resent my minute participation
in that film more than I resent his unwillingness to give me
any credit. He seemed to resent the fact that *anyone* has ever

helped him. . . . That's Steve's problem. That's not my problem.

> Paul Schrader, writer of the
> first screenplay for *Close*
> *Encounters of the Third Kind*
> *circa 1983*

Who the hell had arranged the rooms! Wasn't I as good as Bogie!

> Katharine Hepburn recalling
> her reaction on finding that
> Humphrey Bogart's hotel
> room was better than hers
> during the filming of *The*
> *African Queen*
> *circa 1987*

Heroes and Villains

The frothy, unreal picture is doomed. I knew that for a long time the picture public has liked to think that the hero can do no wrong. But that's an illusion which can't last forever. I think it's riding to a fall now.

> Lois Weber, silent screen
> director
> *1917*

In a movie . . . the hero, as well as the heroine, has to be a virgin. The villain can lay anybody he wants, have as much fun as he wants, cheating and stealing, getting rich and whipping the servants. But you have to shoot him in the end.

> Herman J. Mankiewicz
> *1927*

It is true that we don't want to play him as tough as he [James Cagney] usually plays these things, as there is naturally an objection to slugging dames and all of that stuff today, but, at the same time, we don't want to lose Cagney's real characterization, which is a semi-tough character.

> Hal B. Wallis on Cagney's
> character in *The St. Louis Kid*
> *1934*

It was such a morale booster for us when we most needed it. We had no idea that we were quite so brave.

> The Queen Mother to Greer
> Garson, on seeing *Mrs.*
> *Miniver*
>> *circa 1940s*

There is no confict? These people are fighting for their happiness! Where is the villain? Well, the villain is New York!! What more do you want?!

> Arthur Freed defending *Meet*
> *Me in St. Louis* to MGM
> executives
>> *circa 1942*

When Ford made the V-8, which was sufficiently powerful to outrun the local police automobiles, gangs began to spring up. And that was literally the genesis of the Bonnie and Clyde gang. . . . [I]n American mythology the automobile replaced the horse. This was the transformation of the Western into the gangster.

> Arthur Penn, director of
> *Bonnie and Clyde*
>> *circa 1960s*

We've had a lot of people who were supposed to be great heroes, and you know damn well they weren't. But it's good for the country to have heroes to look up to.

> John Ford
>> *1966*

The first shots of the film show me without the familiar lock of hair across the forehead that was almost Hitler's trademark. I didn't want the audience to start out by saying, "There he is, old Hitler."

> Alec Guinness on developing a new approach to playing the lead in *Hitler: The Last Ten Days*
>
> *circa 1970s*

I've always had a feeling of responsibility towards the image that I'm creating, and if I'm moving in with Lana Turner and going to bump off her husband, then this isn't the image I want. I wanted *The Virginian*; I wanted *Union Pacific*; I wanted to be the guy who rode off into the sunset— "right" over "evil."

> Joel McCrea on turning down the lead in *The Postman Always Rings Twice*
>
> *circa 1970s*

I was ashamed of what Stepin Fetchit and Louise Beavers [black actors] had to do, always playing the low-down parts. . . . [I] knew that if I ever got to be a director, I would try to help get rid of this stigma. . . . *Shaft* comes out a marvelous hero that both black and white kids can look up to as a great guy.

> Gordon Parks, director of *Shaft*
>
> *circa 1971*

So many black characters in movies are actually extensions of a white man's imagination. This one would have been, too, if it wasn't for the fact that we had a black director.

> Richard Roundtree on *Shaft*,
> directed by Gordon Parks
> *circa 1971*

Harry is my favorite role to date. That's the type of thing I like to think I can do as well as, or maybe better than, the next guy.

> Clint Eastwood on *Dirty
> Harry*
> *1974*

After we made that picture, the PTA and the church, the Catholic church, put up a big fuss. They didn't want to see that revenge motive any more than they wanted to see us heroes smoke or drink.

> Charles Starrett, the "Durango
> Kid," on the hero's quest for
> vengeance in *The Outlaws of
> the Prairies*
> *circa 1976*

[Travis] Bickle is somewhere between Charles Manson and Saint Paul.

> Martin Scorsese on the main
> character in *Taxi Driver*
> *circa 1978*

The minute he put on the costume, this tall, skinny kid just decided he could do it. He really felt he could put on the weight and build up. And he did.

> Richard Donner on casting
> Christopher Reeve as
> Superman
> *1979*

What a name for a heavy! I never got over it!

> Lee Marvin on the name
> Liberty Valance
> *circa 1979*

The camera said it [the grapefruit] hit my face, but it didn't. Honey, it's a sin for one actor to hurt another.

> Mae Clarke on the famous
> grapefruit attack by James
> Cagney in *The Public Enemy*
> *circa 1980s*

Bill Wellman, the director . . . took him [Cagney] aside and said, "Look, kid, this will be the most important scene in the picture and you can't fake it." . . . And so the expression of surprise on Mae's face was genuine.

> John Bright, cowriter of *The
> Public Enemy*, on the
> grapefruit attack
> *circa 1980s*

I don't know what a hero is, and I'm sure "heroes" don't know either.

> Harrison Ford
> *circa 1983*

I waste about as much time thinkin' about "the right stuff" as you wasted askin' the question.

> Chuck Yeager, asked what the "stuff" in the movie *The Right Stuff* is
> *1983*

I can shoot a guy in the back, but [John] Wayne can't.

> Clint Eastwood
> *circa 1984*

Hollywood

Millions are to be grabbed out here and your only competition is idiots. Don't let this get around.

> Herman J. Mankiewicz,
> screenwriter, encouraging
> Ben Hecht to come out to
> Hollywood
> *circa 1925*

There is the continual sunlight, the advertised palms, coolness the minute the sun sets, and plenty of people with colds. The boys go around without hats. They look like prize ears of corn. The girls, ditto.

> Stephen Vincent Benét on
> Hollywood
> *circa 1930s*

I just got $11,000 for playing a heavy in a Western—$11,000. No actor is worth that. I got myself a room in a house at the top of Vine Street, I got a secondhand Ford, and I'm not buying anything you can't put on the Chief, because this isn't going to last.

> Clark Gable
> *circa 1930s*

I like every damned thing about the place. Palms and brown hills and boulevards and geraniums six feet tall and flowers running riot everywhere and the grand roads and the golfing and the picture people and even the work, grinding as it is. I like it! Why the hell shouldn't I?

> Katharine Hepburn
> *circa 1930s*

I'm not a little girl from a little town makin' good in a big town. I'm a big girl from a big town makin' good in a little town.

> Mae West on her move from
> Broadway to Hollywood
> *1932*

It was quite unusual to see lights in any windows after ten or ten-thirty.

> William C. De Mille on
> Hollywood in the early 1900s
> *1939*

I've been to Paris, France, and I've been to Paris, Paramount. I think I prefer Paris, Paramount.

> Ernst Lubitsch
> *circa 1930s*

Never in my life have I seen so many unhappy men making a hundred thousand dollars a year.

> Nicholas M. Schenck, MGM
> president
> *circa 1940s*

When I remember this desperate, lie-telling, dime-hunting Hollywood I knew only a few years ago, I get a little homesick. It was a more human place than the paradise I dreamed of and found.

Marilyn Monroe

circa 1950s

In Hollywood a girl's virtue is much less important than her hairdo.

Marilyn Monroe

circa 1950s

I believe that God felt sorry for actors, so he created Hollywood to give them a place in the sun and a swimming pool. The price they had to pay was to surrender their talent.

Sir Cedric Hardwicke

circa 1961

I don't think there'll be a Hollywood as we know it when this generation of film students gets out of college.

Francis Ford Coppola

1968

I was like a kept woman during my twenty-one years at MGM. Hollywood was like an expensive, beautifully run club. You didn't need to carry money. Your face was your credit card—all over the world.

Walter Pidgeon

1969

Economically, the Depression had little effect on the people in Hollywood, most of whom never even got near knowing how to spell it.

> Donald Ogden Stewart,
> screenwriter
> *circa 1969*

There only was Hollywood. The other places to make movies—Paris, for example—were good, but if a French director got the chance to go to Hollywood, he *went*.

> Ingrid Bergman
> *1972*

From the time you were signed at MGM you just felt you were in God's hands.

> Ann Rutherford
> *1975*

It is a tremendous playground, and a lot of people want to get in and play.

> Brian DePalma
> *circa 1978*

I used to dream of being normal. For me, if Sammy Davis or Kirk Douglas walked into the house, that was normal. So the outside world seemed exotic to me. And when I first moved out of our home in Benedict Canyon, I moved to a little house in the San Fernando Valley. That was my dream —a home in suburbia.

> Jamie Lee Curtis, daughter of
> Tony Curtis and Janet Leigh
> *circa 1984*

Los Angeles is where you have to be if you want to be an actor. You have no choice. You go there or New York. I flipped a coin about it. It came up New York, so I flipped again. When you're starting out to be an actor, who wants to go where it's cold and miserable and be poor there?

Harrison Ford

circa 1984

I can remember playing in the Beverly Hills park with Mia Farrow and Candy Bergen and Tish Sterling, and while we sat in the sandbox we could hear our English nannies talking about picture deals and costume direction and whose employer was going to win the Academy Award.

Liza Minnelli

circa 1984

Hollywood is chaos. There's no system; there's no agreement among the people in power—it's all chaos. They're just operating out of fear and ignorance.

Lawrence Kasdan

circa 1985

Hollywood is the only town where everybody at least *thinks* they're cute.

John Waters

1985

The fact that Fritz Lang had made many films in Hollywood, and many very good ones—but no great ones—struck a warning note. If the maker of *Metropolis* and of *Dr. Mabuse* was not allowed to have a free hand in Hollywood, who could?

> Michael Powell on the effect
> of Hollywood's studio system
> on foreign directors
> *circa 1986*

I only go to Los Angeles when I am paid for it.

> Robert De Niro
> *1987*

Lovers

You're a hell of a sheik.

> Young woman ejected from
> Rudolph Valentino's bedroom
> after having broken in to try to
> sleep with him
> > *circa 1920s*

And now do I act like a pink powder puff?

> Rudolph Valentino on his
> deathbed, referring to attacks
> on his virility
> > *1926*

This is the most solemn moment of my life. My innocence of the hideous charge preferred against me has been proved. . . . I am truly grateful to my fellow men and women. My life has been devoted to the production of clean pictures for the happiness of children. I shall try to enlarge my field of usefulness so that my art shall have a wider service.

> Fatty Arbuckle on his
> acquittal for manslaughter on
> the death of Virginia Rappe
> > *1922*

Blonde, pneumatic, and full of peasant health. Just the type meant for me.

> George Sanders proposing
> marriage to Marilyn Monroe
> *circa 1940s*

I saw your test [for *To Have and Have Not*]. We're gonna have a lotta fun together.

> Humphrey Bogart to Lauren
> Bacall
> *circa 1944*

He was a pushover.

> Lauren Bacall on Humphrey
> Bogart
> *circa 1960s*

When two people are falling in love with each other, they're not tough to get along with.

> Howard Hawks on Humphrey
> Bogart and Lauren Bacall in
> *To Have and Have Not*
> *circa 1970s*

It is difficult enough making friends with your own sex, let alone deciding to spend your life with someone of the opposite sex. It is not easy to be interested—and marriage means to be interested—in someone else all the time.

> Katharine Hepburn
> *circa 1950*

To most men I'm a nuisance because I'm so busy I get to be a pest, but Spencer is so masculine that once in a while he rather smashes me down, and there's something nice about me when I'm smashed down.

> Katharine Hepburn
> *circa 1950s*

I can get a divorce whenever I want to. But my wife and Kate like things just as they are.

> Spencer Tracy to Joan Fontaine
> *circa 1950s*

That was something I had never planned on or dreamed about—becoming the wife of a great man. Any more than Joe had ever thought of marrying a woman who seemed 80 percent publicity.

> Marilyn Monroe on marrying Joe DiMaggio
> *circa 1950s*

A GI or Marine or sailor went out at night sparking, and the next day he reported to his cronies, who asked him how he made out, and the fellow said, with a sly grin, *I'm in like Flynn.*

> Errol Flynn on the new idiomatic expression that arose after his acquittal on charges of statutory rape
> *1959*

"We don't want to become another Laurel and Hardy."
"Why? What's so bad about Laurel and Hardy?"

> Richard Burton and Elizabeth
> Taylor
> *circa 1960s*

The real story is that Richard Burton and I are in love, and Elizabeth Taylor is being used as our cover-up.

> Joseph L. Mankiewicz,
> director, on the set of
> *Cleopatra*
> *circa 1962*

She is famine, fire, destruction, and plague; she is the Dark Lady of the Sonnets, the onlie true begetter. She is a secret wrapped in an enigma inside a mystery.

> Richard Burton on his first
> impression of Elizabeth
> Taylor
> *1965*

Don't get into one of your death moods; we'll have it for the rest of the day.

> Elizabeth Taylor to Richard
> Burton
> *circa 1965*

LOVERS

If I found a man who had $15,000,000, would sign over half of it to me before the marriage, and guarantee he'd be dead within a year.

> Bette Davis, asked if she
> would contemplate another
> marriage
> *circa 1960s*

It really shook me up when Trigger passed on. It was like losing one of the family.

> Roy Rogers
> *circa 1966*

My dear, he would have your hand while looking into your eyes and be rubbing his leg on somebody else's leg at the same time, while having the gate man phone him before his wife arrived.

> Joan Blondell on notorious
> rake Leslie Howard
> *1970*

When I went to Italy and stayed there, they [the Hollywood gossip columnists] were delighted, because for ten years they'd wanted to get something on me. And they certainly did. All hell broke up. Louella Parsons was the first one. She said she cried over her typewriter when she had to write the news that I was delivering a son! I think they were tears of joy.

> Ingrid Bergman on her out-of-
> wedlock child by Roberto
> Rosselini
> *1972*

Many people thought we were married.

> Groucho Marx on his
> partnership with Margaret
> Dumont
> *circa 1973*

You should see us when we get back to the bedroom.

> Paul Newman on the success
> of Newman-Woodward
> collaborations
> *1974*

He and Beatty have contests about it.

> Bruce Dern on Jack
> Nicholson's and Warren
> Beatty's womanizing
> *circa 1975*

We wanted to do a good man-woman story [*Chinatown*], and I had Ali [McGraw] in mind—at that time I was married to her. Well, in the interim she left me, so it wasn't for her.

> Robert Evans
> *circa 1975*

I'm oversexed and impotent.

> Sean Connery, commenting
> facetiously on his vices
> *1976*

Jack [John] Ford's idea of a love story is Ward Bond and John Wayne.

> Philip Dunne, screenwriter
> *circa 1978*

We used to call Nelson [Eddy] the singing capon, and her [Jeanette MacDonald] the iron butterfly—two sexless people. They respected each other, but there was no sex in either one of them.

> John Lee Mahin, screenwriter
> *circa 1978*

I'm not too choosy as long as she doesn't have big feet.

> Eddie Murphy on the women
> he's attracted to
> *1983*

Headquarters would close down every afternoon between four and four-thirty. That was [Darryl] Zanuck's playtime. He had a constant stream of women eager to award their favors because he had so many favors to give in return.

> Milton Sperling, Warner Bros.
> executive
> *circa 1984*

When Stewart Granger . . . saw Jean [Simmons] eating a squashy fruit with a ring through her nose [in *Black Narcissus*], he went straight out, proposed to her, and married her. I always said it was the baggy umbrella she carried. It was the final erotic touch.

> Michael Powell
> *circa 1986*

I hate to think of a world without Jack. It would be dismal.

> Anjelica Huston on Jack
> Nicholson
> *1988*

I can't come up with words poetic enough to describe her. She had a very strong aura. She struck me as being stunning. Not pretty, but very beautiful in a powerful way. Deep class.

> Jack Nicholson on Anjelica
> Huston
> *circa 1989*

I was present when the police came. It was not a legal entry.

> Anjelica Huston on Roman
> Polanski's arrest for statutory
> rape while in Jack Nicholson's
> house
> *circa 1989*

Moguls and Producers

If you are going to do anything in this world, you must start before you are forty, before your period of initiative has ended. Do it now!

> Robert H. Cochrane,
> colleague, giving the advice
> that drove unemployed
> clothing store manager Carl
> Laemmle into movies
> *circa 1906*

"I've got the name," [Carl Laemmle] said. . . . "Universal. That's what we're supplying—universal entertainment for the universe."

After the meeting . . . [he explained], "I was looking down on the street as a covered truck went by. On the top was painted 'Universal Pipe Fittings.' "

> Carl Laemmle naming his
> new film company
> *circa 1911*

"Yulius, vat's de matter ve don't get [Adolph] Zukor's prices for our pictures?"

"If we had good pictures, we'd get good prices, but the truth is, Mr. Laemmle, our pictures are lousy."

"Well, Yulius, if you can't get the prices, you get the wolume."

> Carl Laemmle and his
> assistant sales manager, Jules
> Levey
>
> *circa 1920s*

Even the men who hate him cannot despise him.

> Robert H. Cochrane on
> associate Carl Laemmle
>
> *1931*

I will make only pictures that I won't be ashamed to have my little children see. I'm determined that my little Edie and my little Irene will never be embarrassed. And they won't, if all my pictures are moral and clean.

> Louis B. Mayer
>
> *circa 1920s*

I worship good women, honorable men, and saintly mothers.

> Louis B. Mayer
>
> *circa 1920s*

Mr. Zukor enjoys power. There would come a time when he would put his two clenched fists together and, slowly separating them, say to me, "Cecil, I can break you like that."

> Cecil B. De Mille on Adolph
> Zukor
>
> *1959*

I have just finished reading the [Sergei M.] Eisenstein adaptation of *An American Tragedy*. It was for me a memorable experience; the most moving script I have ever read. . . . When I had finished it, I was so depressed that I wanted to reach for the bourbon bottle. As entertainment, I don't think it has one chance in a hundred.

David O. Selznick

1930

You dumb son of a bitch, if you had any brains, you'd still be running Paramount instead of working for me.

Harry Cohn to B. P.
Schulberg, former head of
production at Paramount
circa 1930s

On your first day there [at Columbia], you were invited to lunch with Harry Cohn in the executive dining room. When you came in, there were all the top people of Columbia sitting around. You sat down. Harry Cohn said, "How wonderful to see you, Charles. Welcome!" At which point he pressed a button, and the chair under you collapsed—and you fell on your ass. And everybody laughed, laughed, laughed. This was evidently the greatest joke in the world, that Harry Cohn could collapse a chair under his latest writer.

Charles Bennett

circa 1985

"The boy is a genius. I can see it. I know it."
"Geniuses we have all we need."

Cecil B. De Mille and Jesse
Lasky on Irving Thalberg
circa 1930s

He [Jack L. Warner] was raised in Ohio, and he didn't have the advantages of such a good education.

> Harry Warner apologizing for
> his brother Jack's behavior
> *circa 1930s*

I have a theory of relatives, too. Don't hire 'em.

> Jack L. Warner to Albert
> Einstein
> *circa 1930s*

Jack Warner is a man who would rather tell a bad joke than make a good movie.

> Jack Benny
> *circa 1940s*

He [Jack L. Warner] had a rapierlike wit at the expense of the absent. Nobody left the dining room until after he did— and not out of respect.

> Jack Warner, Jr.
> *circa 1984*

I AM GETTING TO THE END OF THE ROPE OF PATIENCE WITH CRITICISM BASED ON ASSUMPTION THAT ACTORS KNOW MORE ABOUT SCRIPTS THAN I DO.

> David O. Selznick
> *1936*

MOGULS AND PRODUCERS

I started Columbia with spit and wire and these fists, made one-reel comedies with no money to pay bills. I stole, cheated, beat people's brains out . . . got known as a crude, loudmouth son of a bitch. But I built Columbia. Into a major studio. . . . Columbia is—is—not just my love. It's my baby, my *life*. I'd die without Columbia!

> Harry Cohn, in a plea to
> Frank Capra to have him drop
> a lawsuit against Columbia for
> having advertised Capra as
> the director of a non-Capra
> film
> *circa 1937*

NINETY-NINE DIRECTORS OUT OF A HUNDRED ARE WORTHLESS AS PRODUCERS, PARTICULARLY FOR THEMSELVES.

> David O. Selznick
> *1937*

The motion picture represents right and wrong, as the Bible does. By showing both right and wrong, we teach the right.

> Harry Warner on the
> educational qualities of
> Warner Bros. films
> *circa 1937*

Listen, a picture, all it is, is an expensive dream. Well, it's just as easy to dream for $700,000 as for $1,500,000.

> Harry Warner
> *1937*

We are a business concern and not patrons of the arts.

David O. Selznick

1938

I was always an independent, even when I had partners.

Sam Goldwyn

circa 1940s

"And now I should like to bid farewell to my good friend Joe McCrail—"
"Sam—it's McCrea—"
"I've been paying him $5,000 a week for seven years and you're trying to tell me his name?"

Sam Goldwyn and an aide
circa 1940s

I make my pictures to please myself.

Sam Goldwyn

circa 1940s

When I went to Paramount I found, to my joy, a memo paradise.

David O. Selznick on his
years there in the late 1920s
circa 1940s

"Duke, you've been avoiding me."
"That's right."
"What happened, Duke? What went wrong?"
"Jack, it's very simple; you screwed me."

"Duke, I know, but that would have happened anyway. And we're your friends."

Jack L. Warner and John
Wayne
circa 1940s

You don't want to go to Europe. I've just come from Europe, and there's nothing there.

Harry Cohn
circa 1950s

Nicholas M. Schenck never gets his picture in the papers, and he doesn't go to parties, and he avoids going out in public, but he's the *real* king of the pack.

John Huston on the president
of MGM
circa 1950s

Great films, successful films, are made in their *every detail* according to the vision of one man.

David O. Selznick
1962

I told him [Louis B. Mayer] after I had been with the studio about a year that I didn't want a film career. . . . He said, "Here we are making you a big star and you tell me you don't want to be one. You ungrateful little bitch!" . . . I said, "It's you who's the son of a bitch and a pants-presser, too!" . . . Then he had one of his famous heart attacks. . . . Later on I found out that he had them with everybody when he couldn't get his own way.

Kathryn Grayson
circa 1969

I said, "I want to write and direct," and [Louis B.] Mayer said, "No! You have to produce *first*. You have to *crawl* before you walk"—which is as good a definition of producing as I'd ever heard, to this day.

> Joseph L. Mankiewicz
> *circa 1971*

The producer is an authoritarian figure who risks nothing, presumes to know public taste, and always wants to change the end of the film.

> Federico Fellini
> *1972*

[Darryl F. Zanuck] knew the business. When I'd finished a picture, I could go off to Catalina on my boat and fish. Didn't have to hang around. I could leave the editing to him. None of the others knew anything.

> John Ford
> *1973*

He let people alone.

> Irving Berlin on producer
> Arthur Freed
> *circa 1975*

It was said that every evening he [Harry Cohn] personally toured his big studio, trying to catch anyone who might have left on a light.

> Jesse Lasky, Jr.
> *circa 1975*

Harry Warner would go around and kill the lights in the toilets because that's the kind of boss he was.

> Billy Wilder on cost-cutting
> measures at Warner Bros.
> *circa 1988*

I wouldn't ———on them if they were on fire.

> Sean Connery on the
> producers of the Bond films
> *1976*

Sometimes, when we were working on them, we weren't even sure what the project was, because there would be no title. We'd just be shooting the filler material—people in corridors, odd fragments of sex or violence, cars or something. Anything to reach the right length for TV.

> Gary Kurtz on making movies
> with Roger Corman
> *circa 1978*

When the major studios began to do a similar type of film, they couldn't really call them exploitation. . . . More recently they've been called "high-concept films." I like the words "high concept" very much.

> Roger Corman
> *circa 1985*

I thought I might be a ticket-taker at Disneyland or something.

> George Lucas on his
> professional expectations
> while in film school
> *circa 1978*

[Walt Disney] liked people he knew. That's why he kept those same people around him for years and years, that nucleus, and they're still there! Once you became a member of the Disney family you didn't leave! He might destroy you and throw you out in the street at his whim, but no one ever thought of leaving.

William S. Roberts,
screenwriter

circa 1978

[Darryl F. Zanuck] was personally a tinpot Mussolini and an egomaniac, but professionally he was the one producer who respected writers.

John Bright, screenwriter
circa 1980s

Mr. [Louis B.] Mayer was the beating heart of MGM. . . . His birthday was a big fiesta for us. Judy Garland sang, Jeanette MacDonald sang, Mickey Rooney clowned, and we cheered and cheered. . . . There was a strong air of paternalism and it was genuine.

Greer Garson
circa 1980s

At Warner Bros. we were made to toe the line. We were never allowed to be late. Jack Warner kept a record of the first take in the morning and at what hour it was in the can. . . . If you goofed, that was a black mark.

Virginia Mayo
circa 1980s

He [Louis B. Mayer] certainly cried at movies. He cried at *Lassie*, cried at *The Human Comedy*. He cried at *The Great Caruso*.

Danny Selznick

circa 1980s

[Jack L. Warner] took people that you'd never think would be movie stars—Jimmy Cagney, Edward G. Robinson, Humphrey Bogart, Georgie Raft: a strange kind of group. Yet he'd bounce that off with one of the most beautiful men we've ever had in Hollywood, Errol Flynn. That was his way of doing it. MGM did it with beautiful women and beautiful men.

George Sidney, director

circa 1980s

Every morning we'd come in [to the set of *The Blackboard Jungle*] and someone had washed the light switch. I said, "What the hell are we doing? There are supposed to be fingerprints there—these kids use the light switch; don't wash it off." . . . Finally I get a call from Mr. [Louis B.] Mayer, who said, "Don't you understand? We don't have fingerprints in an *MGM movie*."

Richard Brooks

1982

[Howard] Hughes was very standoffish. He always had six or seven men between him and you. I did *Scarface* and he liked what I did; and then I didn't hear from him for twenty years.

W. R. Burnett, screenwriter

circa 1982

I *was* rather in awe of David. He was precociously mature. . . . He was going to bed with girls when I was buggering off.

> Niven Busch, screenwriter, of
> boyhood friend David O.
> Selznick
>
> *1983*

He liked to be the biggest bug in the manure pile.

> Elia Kazan on Harry Cohn
> *circa 1984*

Harry [Cohn] did wonderful things. But he didn't want anyone to know. If he did anything nice, if he helped somebody with money, he wouldn't tell. He'd probably say something nasty about that person.

> Evelyn Keyes, actress
> *circa 1980s*

Underneath [Harry Cohn] had great respect for artists, as he always said, "I kiss the feet of artists." I think a couple of writers came in barefoot one day, and reminded him of his words.

> Daniel Taradash, screenwriter
> *circa 1978*

[Harry Cohn] rated writers and directors by their guts, on the raw theory that creators with mettle knew more about what they were doing than the gentle, sensitive kind.

> Frank Capra
>
> *1971*

He put more people in the cemetery than all the rest of them combined.

> Daniel Fuchs, writer, on
> Harry Cohn
>
> *1962*

[Harry Cohn] seemed to be putting on a kind of act. His son-of-a-bitchery never quite hurt as much as it should have. He could growl or raise hell, and yet the writer or actor or whoever could get along with him.

> James M. Cain
>
> *circa 1976*

Harry Cohn was a bastard, but he was an honest bastard and you knew where you stood with him. He was tough and he made good pictures. . . . That's a mogul that should be around today. Unfortunately, the people today running the studios are to a large degree businessmen—they're not creative; they don't know how to handle people. They're con men, but they're not good con men. . . . You know, they just offend people.

> Sidney Sheldon
>
> *circa 1978*

There was a basic, almost unrealistic resentment when the receipts from *The Sting* and *Jaws* came in and they [my mother and sisters] realized that I had amassed more money with one or two pictures than my father had in a lifetime of work. . . . My bank account changed, but I didn't. But their attitude toward me changed. It went beyond envy. A *dislike* set in.

> Richard D. Zanuck
>
> *circa 1984*

David O. Selznick ... was a big man in every sense. He thought big, he talked big, he was big, but he wasn't quite as big as he thought.

> Michael Powell
>
> *circa 1986*

David [O. Selznick] decided he would like a game of gin rummy. He telephoned for three of these aides of Mr. Mayer, and they, grumbling, got out of bed and came to the studio and played gin until four in the morning. The thought of such power in the hands of such men was bloodcurdling.

> Michael Powell
>
> *circa 1986*

He would pace. Watch television. Get up from the television set. Sit back down in front of the television.

> Danny Selznick on Louis B. Mayer's activities in retirement
>
> *1988*

Like Knute Rockne without a football team to coach.

> David O. Selznick on Louis B. Mayer after being fired from MGM
>
> *1960*

You're nothing if you don't have a studio. Now I'm just another millionaire, and there are a lot of them around.

> Jack L. Warner after his retirement
>
> *circa 1960s*

Are you crazy? If I sell the company, who's going to call me on the telephone?

> Harry Cohn on an offer to buy
> Columbia Pictures
> *circa 1950*

He [David O. Selznick] was hoping for Academy Awards across the board [for *A Farewell to Arms*], and I don't even know if there were any nominations. . . . I said to myself, "Look at what the film industry does to you. It eats you up and spits you out finally. Here's a man who was a genius and a giant in the industry, and he's lost it somehow."

> Danny Selznick
> *circa 1984*

I have learned that *nothing matters but the final picture.*

> David O. Selznick
> *1957*

The Movie Business

It is the crown and flower of nineteenth-century magic, the crystallization of eons of groping enchantments. In its wholesome, sunny, and accessible laws are possibilities undreamt of by the occult lore of the east.

> W. K. L. [William Kennedy
> Laurie] and Antonia Dickson
> on the first movie camera, the
> kinetograph
>
> *1895*

It has long been a source of wonder to me that many women have not seized upon the wonderful opportunities offered to them by the motion picture art to make their way to fame and fortune as producers of photodramas. Of all the arts, there is probably none in which they can make such splendid use of the talents so much more natural to a woman than to a man and so necessary to its perfection.

> Alice Guy-Blaché, director
> *1914*

The end of it will be that the exhibitors will leave off trying to educate the house and give them what they want, which is pictures at twenty-five cents, without musical culture or uplift.

Los Angeles Times reporter on
the rising costs of running
movie palaces

1921

From a production standpoint, you can count on it that Metro-Goldwyn-Mayer will reach a point of perfection never approached by any other company. . . . If there is one thing that I insist upon, it is quality.

Louis B. Mayer

1924

MGM was a studio that spent. It was a studio of white telephones. Warners had black telephones.

Milton Sperling, Warner Bros.
executive

circa 1980s

Let Rembrandt make character studies, not Columbia.

Harry Cohn

circa 1930s

Working for Warner Bros. is like fucking a porcupine—it's one hundred pricks against one.

Wilson Mizner, screenwriter
circa 1930s

"But that's the president's name. You wouldn't name a god-damn actor Abraham Lincoln, would you?"

"No, kid, we wouldn't, because Abe is a name that most people would say is Jewish, and we wouldn't want people to get the wrong idea."

> John Garfield and a Warner
> Bros. executive on the
> suggestion that he call himself
> James Garfield
> *circa 1930s*

A producer told me that the success of *Little Women* was due to the fact that the public was beginning to demand costume plays. Ridiculous! As if the public all got together and passed a resolution demanding costume plays.

> King Vidor
> *1934*

That evening Hollywood was shaken like no earthquake ever shook it. Newspaper headlines carried the startling news that Irving Thalberg fired Von Stroheim. . . . [T]hat was the beginning of the storm and the end of the reign of the director, the mighty oak. The storm grew fiercer. Following the birth of the first producer, Irving Thalberg, came others . . . and when the storm subsided there was no D. W. Griffith, no [James] Cruze, no [Erich] Von Stroheim, no [Rex] Ingram.

> Lewis Milestone
> *1937*

Not all studios allow retakes, especially not for "technical reasons." That is exactly what the studio calls it when you are artistically not satisfied. . . . But if a kiss or a leg is not shown long enough, then you can be sure of retakes.

> William Dieterle, director
> *1938*

The most important saving to be effected in remaking foreign pictures . . . is in the shooting—by actually duplicating,
as far as is practicable, the cut film. . . . I do not mean to put
the director in a straitjacket, but unless the director is willing
to do a duplicating job . . . then we are better off to get a director who is.

> David O. Selznick on
> remaking the Swedish
> *Intermezzo*
>
> *1938*

"I want a part I'm qualified to play."
"Did you hear that, J.L. [Warner]? That's the first son-of-a-
bitch actor who said he *wasn't* good enough. Any son of a
bitch who'll be that honest, if he doesn't want it, I don't want
him!"

> Joel McCrea and Michael
> Curtiz
>
> *1940s*

Everyone is preaching liberty and freedom, and the actors
are getting to believe it, and therefore want to play only the
parts they want to play.

> Harry Warner
>
> *1944*

As if it would last forever. We are not creating something
that will remain for thousands of years. A picture is not a
pyramid . . . it's more like a feather in a hurricane.

> John P. Fulton, special effects
> man
>
> *1945*

I do not believe the film is in a crisis. I believe it finds itself in puberty, the stage when its voice is changing.

Ingmar Bergman
1947

FROM NUMBER OF SCREENINGS WE HAVE HAD ON THIS PICTURE SO FAR WE CAN TELL THAT MIDDLEBROW AND LOWBROW AUDIENCE LIKE IT. HIGHBROWS DO NOT. SINCE MIDDLEBROWS AND LOWBROWS OUTNUMBER HIGHBROWS THOUSAND TO ONE THIS WOULD NOT SEEM LIKE GREAT COMMERCIAL RISK.

Mort Blumenstock, Warner Bros. executive, on *The Fountainhead*
1949

I'll tell you what the business is going to be like and I'm not going to be in it. The other day an agent was in here representing a star and telling me how to rewrite the script. I threw the son of a bitch out of the office, but he'll be back. The agents and the stars are going to be running the business, and when that happens, I don't want to be here and I'd advise you not to be here either.

Darryl F. Zanuck to Philip Dunne
circa 1950

The movie business is macabre. Grotesque. It is a combination of a football game and a brothel.

Federico Fellini
circa 1950s

The hell where all little movies go when they're bad.

Judy Garland on television
circa 1950s

"I'll send that down to your office."
"Darryl, I haven't even got an office."
"For chrissakes, I keep telling all these people they have to stay in their offices, and you don't even got one. How do you think that looks? You have to *have* an office. You don't have to sit in it."

Darryl F. Zanuck and
screenwriter Philip Dunne
circa 1950s

At this point Jack Warner discovered that by "percentage of the gross" [on *Darby's Rangers*], we actually *meant* just that. He promptly fired me.

Charlton Heston
1957

If I discover that one of my men believes he knows which films will make money and which will lose, I say that he has "gone Hollywood" and I fire him.

Al Howe, banker, on financing
movies
circa 1960s

Some of [my] Columbia pictures were damned good, but I think what screwed them up were the titles. Look at the ones I've been stuck with: *It Should Happen to You, You Can't*

Run Away from It, Phffft! When we were shooting *Phffft!* they stopped production right in the middle of the day so they could discuss that title. Everyone waited while they went into a two-and-a-half-hour huddle upstairs. When they broke, I asked the director about it, and he said they'd decided to take out one "f."

Jack Lemmon
circa 1960s

Some of the downbeat pictures, in my opinion, should never be made at all. Most of them are made for personal satisfaction, to impress other actors who . . . say "Oh, God! what a shot, what camera work!" But the average person in the audience, who bought his ticket to be entertained, doesn't see that at all. He comes out depressed.

Doris Day
1962

We could have been bad actors, it didn't matter. It was the fact of volume . . . you were just shipped everywhere and people got accustomed to that face, like they would get accustomed to the emblem of a Rolls-Royce, that little statue of the lady on the hood.

Gloria Swanson
1964

During the Depression I was making more than six pictures a year. I made six pictures while carrying my son and eight with my daughter. They'd get me behind desks and behind barrels and throw tables in front of me to hide my growing tummy. And I never had more than two weeks before starting a picture. I mean, just let me have the poor child and then back to work.

> Joan Blondell
> *1970*

Marty, if you could swing a little and kinda conceive *Mean Streets* as black, we might be able to do it in New York, non-union, shoot it very fast.

> Roger Corman to Martin
> Scorsese, hoping to make
> *Mean Streets* into a black
> exploitation film
> *circa 1973*

One of the first things that happened was that Walter Wanger, who was then in charge of production for Paramount, wanted me to remove my moustache because he didn't think it looked real enough for film.

> Groucho Marx on his debut in
> movies
> *circa 1973*

Sometimes you'd have one director on a picture for a while, and if he got sick, instead of calling the picture off for a week as they would do now if Mike Nichols took ill, they'd say, "Jack Conway isn't well. Let him rest. We'll put Harry Beaumont on it for a week, and he'll pick up where Jack left off." That's the way we made pictures. Of course, it's not the way it's done now.

> Pandro S. Berman, producer
> at MGM
> *circa 1974*

I'm sure I'll have to wind up making my living in that way. All old actors do.

Jack Nicholson on television
circa 1975

Just look at our gods. Look at [Orson] Welles. He's the greatest director in the world, and he can't get a job and he's sold out. Totally. Orson Welles on the Johnny Carson show doesn't give us much to hope for. That is the story of this business.

Brian DePalma
circa 1978

The creation of a painting, say, or a sculpture, implies the existence of a single creator, but it is beyond some of the critics to contemplate the possibility of a collaborative art for the movies—it's like building a Chartres cathedral; so they must unearth an author, a single individual who can be credited with the entire concept, but the motion picture is not like a painting; it's more like a building.

Philip Dunne
circa 1978

Distribution [of films] is a freemasonry like the kitchens of a restaurant. They have deep, dark secrets. I have never yet been able to discover how much it costs to distribute a film.

Alfred Hitchcock
circa 1978

Nobody in a studio challenges the final cut of a film now. I think they realize the filmmakers are likely to be around a lot longer than the studio executives. Now, power lies with the filmmakers, and we are the group that is getting the power.

John Milius
circa 1978

The first time I was ever plonked into a makeup chair at MGM, the head of makeup looked me over and said, "Well, who is she? Is she Garbo? Hardly. Is she Jeanette Mac-Donald? Hardly. Is she Norma Shearer?" I said, "Couldn't I just be Greer Garson?"

Greer Garson
circa 1980s

A "B" picture isn't a big picture that just didn't grow up; it's exactly what it started out to be. It's the $22 suit of the clothing business; it's the hamburger of the butchers' shops; it's a seat in the bleachers—and there's a big market for all of them.

Nick Grinde, "B"-movie
director
circa 1980s

In every studio head's office there was always a little cupboard in which there was a private telephone. And he'd say, "Excuse me a minute; I have to go and wash my hands," and he'd go into the cupboard and he was really talking to New York. . . . [Louis B. Mayer] had power in a very parochial sense, yes—but only on the lot.

Joseph L. Mankiewicz
circa 1980s

All the fun lies in talking about Louis Mayer did this and Louis Mayer did that, but Louis Mayer fought throughout his life to acquire some power. In the end he was fired by his bosses in New York when they thought he was no longer any use to them.

Joseph L. Mankiewicz
circa 1980s

You know, it's all falling apart as we speak; it's ending. The industry is going to fall into the hands of people who are not movie people, and when it does that, it's really going to be in trouble.

Clifford Odets to Peter Bogdanovich on the decline of the studio system
1961

[Movie executives] tell you, "Listen, I've been in the business for thirty years; for God's sake, I know how to look at a movie." Well, my father drove a car for thirty-five years, and he was a lousy driver until the day he died.

Richard Brooks
1982

We're going to make pictures for what they should truly cost, and the emphasis is on adventure, action, and romantic pix hyphenated to comedy. We're not making any downbeat, subjective, introverted, negative character studies.

Freddie Fields, MGM production head
1983

Was I demoralized? You bet I was. Particularly as the studio thought it would be a good idea if I wore my hair like Elvis

Presley and changed my name. I suggested Kurt Affair. After that, there was no more talk of changing names.

> Harrison Ford on being a
> contract player at Columbia
> Pictures in the 1960s
> *circa 1984*

There's a general juvenilization of movies that's happened over the last ten years that's pretty scary. The other day somebody read a script that I was working on and said, "Oh, I get it: This is an adult comedy." I said, "What do you mean—that it's a comedy *for* adults?" He said, "No, no, no—it's a comedy *about* adults."

> Peter Bogdanovich
> *circa 1985*

Everything was in disarray—so disorganized. . . . You really had to make very cautious enquiries, if only at the telephone switchboard, to find out who the president of the company was that week.

> Greer Garson on the decline
> of the studios during the
> 1950s
> *circa 1985*

Nobody sends Christmas cards to a loser.

> George Sidney on Louis B.
> Mayer's isolation after he was
> fired from MGM
> *circa 1985*

It was only the United States that had to be protected from the realities of life and death.

> Michael Powell on being
> forced to change the title of
> the British film *A Matter of
> Life and Death* to *Stairway to
> Heaven* for its American
> release
>
> *circa 1986*

Perhaps all works of art that necessitate a collaboration between an artist and his patron contain within them the seeds of enmity.

> Michael Powell
>
> *circa 1986*

You can have a film and have 200 white people working on it, and nobody finds anything wrong with that. But if you insist on having a black crew, all of a sudden there's something wrong.

> Richard Pryor on his
> insistence on hiring black
> production people
>
> *1986*

I hope that the best of them want to make a good film. But the rest should be bank tellers.

> Kathleen Turner on
> Hollywood executives
>
> *1986*

I hate today's style of production. I understand the time-money equation, but it's a nightmare.... It's like saying to

Van Gogh that the brush strokes don't matter. I mean, sometimes the brush strokes are all that *do* matter!

> George A. Romero
> *circa 1987*

Then the telephone rang. Well, that's what happens in our business.

> Katharine Hepburn on the call
> that resulted in her starring in
> *The African Queen*
> *1987*

As long as kids want to get away from home, as long as they want to have a nice place to neck, as long as kids can't stand their parents, movies will exist.

> William Goldman
> *circa 1980s*

Musicals

The ideal movie chorine measured a 32½-inch bust, 23-inch waist, 34-inch hips, 12½-inch calf, 7½-inch ankle. Venus de Milo with her 28½-inch waist couldn't get a job as a script girl on poverty row.

> *Photoplay* article on Warner
> Bros. chorus girls
> *1929*

They don't have to be able to sing a note.

> Florenz Ziegfeld on
> qualifications of chorus girls
> *1929*

The first day in, I went to the studio for lunch to meet Mr. [Jack L.] Warner. . . . He sprawled over the table and said, "Well, now you're here, you got to get to work. And I don't vant none of your highbrow song-making. Musik vit guts, ve got to have—songs vit real sendiment like 'Stein Song' and 'Vit Tears in My Eyes, I'm Dencing.'"

It turned out the whole thing had been a put-up joke arranged by the others with Jack Warner.

> Richard Rodgers
> *1930*

Once I had 723 girls show up on a call for one of my Gold Diggers pictures. I was all afternoon picking girls out of this large number, and finally ended up selecting three.... My sixteen regular contract girls were sitting on the side waiting, so after I picked the three girls, I put them next to my special sixteen and they matched, just like pearls.

Busby Berkeley
circa 1930s

I had a simple, corny, well-felt little melodrama, and they made an ill-felt, silly, maudlin, badly timed thing of it.

Samson Raphaelson on the
screen adaptation of his play
The Jazz Singer
circa 1930s

I am a little uncertain about the man, but I feel, in spite of his enormous ears and bad chin line, that his charm is so tremendous that it comes through even in this wretched test.

David O. Selznick on Fred
Astaire's screen test
1933

About the most important part of his work clothes—his shoes—he is extremely careless. One day, they are sport shoes, another brogues, another dancing slippers. When a picture is made, he wears regulation dance pumps with metal plates on heel and toe. He wears size eight and a half, and each pair costs around $20.

Photoplay article on Fred
Astaire
1935

Arthur, I want you to hear a little girl.

> Jack Robbins, head of MGM's
> music-publishing firm, to
> Arthur Freed on Judy Garland
> *1935*

We have problems with the Munchkins. They are so darn small and their costumes are all more or less the same. When they all mob together, they are just a mass of nothing.

> Harold Rosson, cameraman,
> on *The Wizard of Oz*
> *circa 1938*

The song stays—or I go! It's as simple as that.

> Arthur Freed insisting on
> keeping "Over the Rainbow"
> in *The Wizard of Oz*
> *1939*

You're Andy Hardy! You're the United States! You're the Stars and Stripes. Behave yourself! You're a symbol!

> Louis B. Mayer to Mickey
> Rooney
> *circa 1940s*

Oh, hell! Let's just write something about the trolley, and to hell with it!

> Ralph Blane and Hugh
> Martin, struggling to compose
> a song for the trolley scene in
> *Meet Me in St. Louis*
> *circa 1943*

They're not going to get me into another sailor's suit!

> Frank Sinatra after *Anchors Aweigh*
>
> *circa 1945*

The *Red Shoes* girl is a girl like other girls. It's a good story, but there's nothing period about it. We are making this film for a twentieth-century audience with a twentieth-century girl.

> Michael Powell to costume designer Hein Heckroth
>
> *1946*

"Shall I jump like a girl committing suicide, or like a ballerina?"
"Like a ballerina."

> Moira Shearer and Michael Powell on the final scene of *The Red Shoes*
>
> *circa 1946*

When Alex Korda showed the film [*The Red Shoes*] in his private projection room to the King and Queen and the two young princesses, he told me they were all devastated by the ending of the picture . . . and thanked him with tears streaming down their faces for showing them "such a lovely—boo-hoo!—picture."

> Michael Powell
>
> *1986*

I'm tired of playing little girls. I'm a woman now; I can't run around forever being the little Miss Fix-It who bursts into song.

Deanna Durbin

1949

Intimate musical is the only way to get true entertainment. People are not entertained by chorus lines anymore. It's also less expensive and more rewarding to concentrate on the principals.

Roger Edens, associate
producer of *On the Town*
circa 1949

Live people get off a real ship in the Brooklyn Navy Yard and sing and dance down New York City. We did a lot of quick cutting—we'd be on the top of Radio City and then on the bottom . . . and so the dissolve went out of style. This was one of the things that changed the history of musicals more than anything.

Gene Kelly on *On the Town*
circa 1970s

"Now, Gene," I would say, "make it jaunty." Gene, of course, was born jaunty.

Vincente Minnelli on Gene
Kelly in *An American in Paris*
1974

None of us had the courage to say to him [Arthur Freed], "For Christ sake, it obviously works for the number, but it's a stolen song, Arthur."

> Stanley Donen on the striking
> similarity between "Make
> 'Em Laugh" in *Singin' in the*
> *Rain* and Irving Berlin's
> earlier "Be a Clown"
> *circa 1970s*

They thought I was crazy, because I went to the set and had them dig holes in the ground to accumulate the rainwater, to give me puddles, which I would use for certain steps in my dance routine.

> Gene Kelly on *Singin' in the*
> *Rain*
> *circa 1970s*

We knew from the start there was a scene where there was rain, and the leading man was singin' in it. What we hadn't written into the script was: "Here Gene Kelly does perhaps the outstanding solo number of his career."

> Betty Comden and Adolph
> Green, authors of *Singin' in*
> *the Rain*
> *circa 1972*

Suddenly a small lithe figure came sliding across at us like a hockey player zooming over the ice. It was [François] Truffaut himself, and he was breathless and awestruck at meeting the authors of "Chantons sous la Pluie" ["Singin' in the Rain"].

> Betty Comden and Adolph
> Green on visiting Paris
> *circa 1950s*

We were very nervous in the beginning about Fred [Astaire]'s character [in *The Band Wagon*] because it was based in so many ways on his actual position in life.

> Betty Comden
> *circa 1975*

I had always played a bachelor before, but here I was married! And I'd treat her atrociously—just as though she were my real wife!

> Oscar Levant on his character
> in *The Band Wagon*
> *circa 1950s*

"There's nothing the matter with you; it's all in your mind."
"In my mind? What a horrible place to be!"

> Vincente Minnelli and Oscar
> Levant, on the set of *The
> Band Wagon*
> *circa 1952*

I remember *Holiday Inn* because in it Fred Astaire danced himself so thin that I could almost spit through him. In the film he did one number thirty-eight times before he was satisfied with it. He started the picture weighing 140 pounds. When he finished it he weighed 126.

> Bing Crosby
> *1953*

I have no desire to prove anything by it. I have never used it as an outlet or as a means of expressing myself. I just dance.

> Fred Astaire
> *1959*

The Sound of Mucus.

> Christopher Plummer's name
> for *The Sound of Music*
> during the early stages of
> filming
> > *circa 1964*

I don't know what to say, except that it haunts me as an embarrassment of bad taste.

> Roger Edens on the battleship
> finale of *Born to Dance*
> > *circa 1969*

The biggest thing to happen to the MGM musical was the discovery of Judy Garland.

> Roger Edens
> > *circa 1969*   .

Initially, studio executives weren't at all keen on the idea of Judy [Garland] growing up. Mr. Mayer, a very sweet old guy, was in the center of the debate about making Judy both the mother and the daughter [in *Little Nelly Kelly*]. "We simply can't let that baby have a child," he'd say.

> Roger Edens
> > *circa 1969*

One day, when we were doing *Summer Stock*, Judy [Garland] hadn't shown up and it was long past noon. . . . When she arrived she was on the verge of tears as she explained her lateness. That morning, she'd arrived at the studio at 6:00 A.M. for makeup, and instead of reading "MGM" over the studio gates, it read "The time has come." To her it meant that this was the day when she would go on the stage to film and the people would suddenly turn and point, saying, "Who the hell do you think you are? What makes you think you are a good dancer? or that you can sing?" She had been so petrified when she saw this that she turned the car around and drove until she reached the beach, where she tried to sort herself out.

Walter Plunkett
circa 1969

We'd get wild ideas and say, "Let's do it!" and we did!

Charles Walters on directing musicals at MGM
circa 1969

"I was just up with Mr. Curtiz," she [Rosemary Clooney] told me, "and he started to tell me the story of the picture [*White Christmas*]—it was so marvelous—and when he got to a certain point, he was so involved with the story, he actually began to cry a little, and he stopped and said, 'Excuse me, my dear, I simply cannot go on.'"

I didn't tell Rosemary that Mike couldn't go on because Norman and Mel were upstairs and they hadn't sent him the rest of the script yet.

Robert Emmett Dolan, producer, on last-minute script revisions by Norman Panama and Melvin Frank
circa 1970

The toughest one to put over . . . was *Meet Me in St. Louis*, which nobody at the studio liked. Finally we had a meeting and Mayer said: "Arthur's record has been so good, either he'll learn a lesson or we'll learn a lesson. So go make the picture." And it was the biggest-grossing picture they had for five years.

Arthur Freed

1974

"What I want to do is take George [Gershwin]'s composition of 'An American in Paris' and use it *in toto* for the finish of the picture as a ballet."
"Kid, I hope you know what you're doing. To do a twenty-minute ballet in a picture!"

Arthur Freed and Irving
Berlin

1974

When I'd talk to Fred [Astaire] alone, he'd say, "Gene [Kelly] is wonderful, but why does he want everything his own way?" And when I'd see Gene alone, he'd say, "I admire Fred so much, but why does he want everything his own way?"

Arthur Freed on the dancers'
collaboration in *Ziegfeld
Follies*

1974

I had a hell of a time with [MGM studio head] Dore Schary because he wanted me to put Dinah Shore in that part [the one that went to Ava Gardner]. . . . Dinah was sending me flowers to the house and everything . . . and she finally said, "Why don't you give me the part?" And I said: "Because you're not a whore ... Ava is. When she sings 'Bill,' she's every streetwalker you ever saw."

> Arthur Freed on casting *Show Boat*
>
> *1974*

It's much more important to me if they had made the picture. And they could have. It was to be Arthur [Freed]'s and my swan song in motion pictures. But those "civilians," as I call them—the guys in New York—making decisions that should have been made by Arthur Freed. They were stupid!

> Irving Berlin on MGM's 1969 decision to cancel their proposed musical *Say It with Music*
>
> *circa 1975*

Nobody dressed Elvis Presley better than Elvis.

> Edith Head on designing Elvis's movie wardrobe
>
> *circa 1980*

In *Saturday Night Fever* ... in the opening we took a tape recorder out with us in the street—we already had a demo made by the Bee Gees of "Staying Alive." ... Of course, Travolta's feet are going right on the beat. And that makes a big difference.

> John Badham
>
> *1983*

There is marvelous stuff in *Pal Joey*, but the fact is that they go off into the sunset together at the end. That was what I didn't want.

> Martin Scorsese discussing
> *New York, New York*
> *circa 1980s*

WHEN I WAS A BOY IN RUSSIA YOUR POLICE TREATED MY PEO-
PLE VERY BADLY. HOWEVER NO HARD FEELINGS. HEAR YOU ARE
NOW OUT OF WORK. IF YOU COME TO NEW YORK CAN GIVE YOU
FINE POSITION ACTING IN PICTURES.

> Lewis J. Selznick to Czar
> Nicholas II after the Russian
> Revolution
> *circa 1917*

Viewed as drama, the war is disappointing.

> D. W. Griffith on making the
> propaganda film *Hearts of the
> World*, about World War I
> *1918*

Ben-Hur was a great joke on Mussolini. When we went to
Italy to shoot the picture, he was most hospitable. He thought
we were about to re-create the grandeur that was Rome. . . .
[W]hen we were done and had gone home and he saw the
film, he almost had a stroke. The hero was a young Jewish
follower of Christ, and a Roman was the villain of the picture.

> Francis X. Bushman
> *circa 1930s*

I would like to get a good writer to do a little polishing on the script [for *The Dawn Patrol*] and begin planning it for production. . . . We could knock out a very great picture in a very short time, and one that I think would bring us a fortune now when the whole world is talking and thinking war and rearmament.

Hal B. Wallis

1938

Hollywood gave her the cold shoulder. A leading nightclub refused to allow her to enter. None of the major studios would give her a studio pass.

Frank Tuttle on Nazi director
Leni Riefenstahl's visit to
Hollywood

1939

A group of young cartoonists from Hollywood's animated cartoon studios are preparing plans for cartoons to knife the dictators right in their Mickey Mice.

Frank Tuttle on plans for
anti-Axis cartoons

1939

When I made *The Rules of the Game,* I knew where I was going. I knew the evil that gnawed at my contemporaries. . . . I think the film is a good one. But it is not so difficult to work well when the compass of anxiety points in the true direction.

Jean Renoir on making the
film in France just prior to
World War II

circa 1960s

"Jimmy, I see by the papers that you've been a bad boy."
"All I did, Mr. President, was believe in the things you believe."
"Attaboy, Jimmy."

> Franklin Roosevelt to James
> Cagney, who was then under
> investigation for alleged
> Communist ties
>
> *circa 1940*

Messages are for Western Union.

> Sam Goldwyn
>
> *circa 1940s*

Every American citizen ought to be proud of a nation which has an industry working so closely with the Army and thus contributing materially to the national defense program.

> Colonel Clarence R. Huebner,
> chief of the Training Branch
> of the Army, on training films
> produced by the Academy of
> Motion Picture Arts and
> Sciences
>
> *1941*

Somehow, I suppose pictures will be made despite the fact that they are going to have a terrible time finding leading men. . . . [Clark] Gable is a private in the Army; [Tyrone] Power is a private in the Marines; [Henry] Fonda is a gob; [Van] Heflin has been drafted. . . . In the words of Adolphe Menjou, if the thing keeps up, the women stars in pictures will be willing to work with men of their own age.

> David O. Selznick
>
> *1942*

If Bette Davis or anyone else wants to appear at any rally, whether Republican or Democratic, that is their business. People are not going into theaters because Davis is Republican or Democratic, because if that were the case, no one would go see pictures, as any performer is one or the other.

Harry Warner

1944

Members of the Association of Motion Picture Producers deplore the action of the ten Hollywood men who have been cited for contempt. . . . Their actions have been a disservice to their employers and have impaired their usefulness to the industry. We will forthwith discharge or suspend without compensation those in our employ and we will not re-employ any of the ten until such time as he is acquitted or has purged himself of contempt and declares under oath that he is not a Communist.

Statement of the Association
of Motion Picture Producers
circa 1947

"They wanted to know the names of people I thought might be Communists out here."
"What did you say?"
"Well . . . I told them the names of a few."
"You did?"
"Yeah . . . I guess I shouldn't have, should I?"

Jack L. Warner and
John Huston

1947

I wouldn't be allowed to make *The Best Years of Our Lives* in Hollywood today.

> William Wyler on the growing
> suppression of films that
> questioned the established
> order
>
> *1948*

"I wouldn't go around raving about Lincoln Steffens. It's certain to get you into trouble. People will begin to talk of you as a radical."
"A radical what?"

> Joseph L. Mankiewicz and
> Marilyn Monroe discussing a
> book she was reading on the
> set of *All About Eve*
>
> *circa 1949*

For God's sake, I know this guy. He's been a registered Democrat ever since he was old enough to vote. Where the hell do they get off, saying he's a Communist?

> Harry Cohn insisting on
> hiring "gray-listed" director
> Vincent Sherman
>
> *circa 1950*

Senator [Joseph] McCarthy was one of the finest Americans who ever lived.

> John Wayne
>
> *circa 1960s*

I saw him [Charlie Chaplin] in the south of France some years ago, and I remember the subject of communism kept cropping up, and somebody said, "Well, you're supposed to be a Communist," and he said, "I'm not a Communist; I'm an atheist . . . I don't believe in any government!"

> Gloria Swanson
> *1964*

The politicians are secretly terrified that we are all going to run and win.

> Shirley MacLaine on actors
> and politics
> *circa 1970s*

Those who say that it's a fascist film are just reveling in big words.

> Clint Eastwood on critical
> reaction to *Dirty Harry*
> *1977*

I certainly don't think we should have more cops with wider powers on the street. I'm very alarmed at the idea of the police; I don't particularly like the police. I'm a great advocate of the Second Amendment. . . . The Second Amendment is so that if the police become too oppressive, you can shoot them.

> John Milius
> *circa 1980s*

I'm not a political person. I've never been aware of unions or human conditions other than my own. That's a terrible thing to admit, but that's what I am.

> Sally Field while discussing
> *Norma Rae*
> *1979*

The Los Angeles Times, which was an arch-conservative
newspaper at that time, knew enough to write an editorial
against the picture [*The Devil and Miss Jones*]. But the guy
who came from some labor magazine . . . got up at the press
preview in the studio and said, "You copped out." . . . I
looked at this amateur. He hadn't the vaguest idea of how
propaganda works and what social statement I wanted to
make. The editorial writer for *The Los Angeles Times* knew
this was a dangerous picture.

> Norman Krasna, screenwriter,
> *The Devil and Miss Jones*
> *circa 1980*

[Hedda Hopper] had a whole list of movies that were Com-
munist-controlled, with Communist philosophy in them. One
or two were ones where they had a banker who held a mortgage . . . over a poor family. We said, "Jesus, Hedda, a banker
holding a mortgage on a family has been a heavy for five
thousand years! This is not Communist!"

> John Lee Mahin
> *circa 1980*

Finally, when the pressure came on them, this Motion Picture Producers Association, like a tower of jelly, collapsed at
the first touch.

> Philip Dunne on the decision
> of producers not to employ
> people suspected of being
> Communists
> *circa 1980s*

Right up until the last minute I knew what I was doing was
wrong for me, as a human being, and yet I felt myself being
almost inexorably drawn into it. . . . [T]he only thing for me to

do really, since I didn't feel like going to jail, was to go along and be a rat. . . . But I thought then, as I'm thinking now, that I guess it's the only thing I've ever done in my life for which I'm ashamed.

> Sterling Hayden, who named
> names to the House Un-
> American Activities
> Committee
>> *circa 1980s*

   The telephone stopped ringing. That's all. I knew what that meant.

> Howard Koch, blacklisted
> screenwriter
>> *circa 1980s*

   I was asked to come down and see the legal department, and they told me I had to clear myself. And I just didn't. It wasn't bravery or anything at all. I felt and still feel so very proud of those years with the Anti-Nazi League, and to say that I'd been duped into that was just not true. So that was the end of my Hollywood career.

> Donald Ogden Stewart
>> *circa 1985*

Production

A rock is a rock; a tree is a tree—shoot it in Griffith Park!

> The Stern Brothers, uncles of
> Universal studio head Carl
> Laemmle, on location
> shooting
> *circa 1920s*

"Now, Dimitri! Forget Borodin and Moussorgsky. Only native American themes, hear? Folk songs, Stephen Foster, Sousa, W. C. Handy—"

"Fronk, vat you theenk, I'm like children? Papichka, in my head is notes like apple pie so American—"

> Frank Capra and Dimitri
> Tiomkin during the making of
> *Mr. Smith Goes to
> Washington*
> *circa 1938*

What can I do to get you makeup men to throw away your kits and your tweezers? The public is so far ahead of you all and is so sick of your makeup that you are all managing to contribute to the destruction of stars.

> David O. Selznick to Monty
> Westmore, makeup artist
> *1939*

Anybody who can take that makeup every morning deserves respect.

> Boris Karloff on his successors
> in the role of Frankenstein's
> monster
> *circa 1940s*

There are two main motifs [in *Citizen Kane*]. One—a simple four-note figure in the brass—is that of Kane's power. . . . The second motif is that of Rosebud. Heard as a solo on the vibraphone, it first appears during the death scene at the very beginning of the picture. It is heard again and again through the film under various guises, and if followed closely, is a clue to the ultimate identity of Rosebud itself.

> Bernard Herrmann, composer
> *1941*

For some time now I have been noticing that there is something about the recording of the music in Warner Bros. pictures that makes the music infinitely more effective than in our own.

> David O. Selznick
> *1941*

Most of the sound departments and a lot of theater patrons think that the main thing that distinguishes Warner Bros.' music from that of all other companies is the volume of it.

> Ray Klune of David O.
> Selznick Productions
> *1941*

Like most of the early pioneers in films, Jack [Warner] evidently felt that music had a magical mystery power, a subliminal power. So they began to use it indiscriminately. It was like an enema in the Jewish family tradition. "It can't hurt you" was the idea.

> Leonard Rosenman, composer
> *circa 1983*

I am much afraid of [Bette] Davis's hat, where you will have to guess what she is thinking about. A large hat may be all right and again it may not, but we must see the people's eyes when they are acting.

> Jack L. Warner
> *1942*

I do wish we did not have his [Gregory Peck's] hat as far down on his head; and I wish you would tell both King [Vidor] and Greg that the hat has a tendency to make the material look like a double . . . and also I think he is so attractive without his hat that I think we should play more scenes without it.

> David O. Selznick to Hal C.
> Kern, supervising film editor,
> on *Duel in the Sun*
> *1945*

I discovered [when I was a child] that they made dandy bombs when you fill them with water. I used to drop them on top of people from windows. And I remember[ed] that they used to hold a tear-shaped form on their way down.

> Jack Arnold, director of *The Incredible Shrinking Man,* on how he decided to use condoms filled with water to create giant water drops
> *circa 1956*

All it takes is mechanical ability, a knowledge of hydraulics, pneumatics, electronics, engineering, construction, ballistics, explosives, and no acquaintance with the word *impossible.*

> Danny Lee, special effects man
> *circa 1965*

Shoes had to be covered specially with felt and rubber, since without them, the leading lady sounded like an onrushing herd of buffalo when she tiptoed on the set.

> Walter Plunkett, costume designer, on technical problems in early sound films
> *circa 1969*

He [the sound man] was a magician. Nobody understood what he was up to, so he could get away with all sorts of things.

> Douglas Fairbanks, Jr.
> *circa 1980s*

I didn't create a "Garbo face." I just did portraits of her I would have done for any star. My lighting of her was determined by the requirements of a scene. I didn't, as some say I did, keep one side of the face light and the other dark. But I did always try to make the camera peer into the eyes, to see what was there.

William Daniels,
cinematographer
circa 1970

If it's an uninteresting scene, the music can make it so exciting that you think they really said something.

Max Steiner, composer
circa 1970

How could we make a Swede look Oriental?

Frank Capra on makeup for
Nils Asther in *The Bitter Tea
of General Yen*
1971

In California, they like to pigeonhole you. From the time I began working for [Alfred] Hitchcock, they decided I was a big suspense man. On other occasions, I've had fantasies or bittersweet romantic stories. I think I'd enjoy writing a good comedy score, but I've never had the luck to be offered such films . . . Mancini gets the cheerful ones.

Bernard Herrmann, composer
circa 1971

Stephen [Boyd] had to look mangled and beaten up. I made bits of flesh to hang from him, and with all his scars and cuts and chewed-up elbows and blood he looked quite horrible. But Willie Wyler, the director, was still not satisfied. "More blood, more blood," he demanded. "Give *me* the bottle!" Then he threw more of it all over poor Boyd.

> Charles Parker, makeup man
> for the 1959 *Ben-Hur*
> *1972*

I suppose you could describe me as the real Dr. Frankenstein. . . . I build the monsters, cut out brains, sew hands onto dead bodies, and supply all the other gory paraphernalia for the operations.

> Les Bowie, special effects
> man for Hammer's
> *Frankenstein* movies
> *circa 1974*

You read a script and it contains really difficult problems in special effects . . . and you spend two days thinking about them before you suddenly say: "I know how to do that!" And you go back to the production manager and tell him . . . and you should be paid half of your fee for those two days because that's when the real work is done.

> Les Bowie, special effects
> man
> *circa 1974*

I made the leeches for that famous scene where Bogart gets covered with them. At first they had real leeches which were supposed to be stuck on the back of a stunt man, but they wouldn't stick. . . . So I made a Plasticine model of one of the leeches and from that a plaster mold was made. . . . To stick them onto Bogart I used a waterproof adhesive. They had a hell of a job pulling them off, but they worked like a charm.

> Cliff Richardson, special
> effects man on *The African Queen*
> *circa 1974*

The first time I see her [Kim Novak], I see that she has a good bust. She doesn't need padding and all that thing we were doing to everybody. Less shoulder and keep her looking very natural, with nothing, just put the clothes on her and show her bosom; it's moving—it's not a stiff thing like all those girls then.

> Jean Louis, designer
>
> *1977*

Oh, that sweater, I'm so sick of that thing.

> Jean Louis on Lana Turner's famous sweater
>
> *1977*

We looked at every war movie ever made that had air-to-air combat, from *The Blue Max* to *The Battle of Britain*. . . . We were looking for the reason each shot worked, the slight roll of the wings that made it look real.

> Gary Kurtz on designing the dogfights in *Star Wars*
>
> *circa 1978*

[Dorothy Lamour] was . . . self-conscious about her feet. . . . The makeup department concocted some rubber feet which were flawless, and she attempted to wear those with her sarong, but they were so delicate that "new feet" had to be made every day. . . . She eventually kicked them off, accepting the fact that even if her feet weren't as gorgeous as the rest of her, they were functional—and function does have its own rewards.

> Edith Head
>
> *circa 1980*

The off-the-shoulder dress for the big party scene [in *All About Eve*] was an accident. . . . The dress was made up the night before Bette [Davis] was scheduled to wear it. . . . [It] didn't fit at all. . . . Someone had miscalculated and the entire bodice and neckline were too big. . . . She pulled the neckline off her shoulders, shook one shoulder sexily, and said, "Don't you like it better like this, anyway?"

Edith Head

circa 1980

When the girls come in for fittings now, they come in jeans, and many of them don't even bother with underwear. No more Grace Kelly with white gloves.

Edith Head

circa 1980

Fittings can take hours with women, but on this film [*The Sting*] it took only an hour to dress the world's two handsomest men.

Edith Head

circa 1980

People would just start showing up, and we'd put them through a makeup assembly line. We pulled in something like 1,500 zombies, which is pretty astronomical! *Everyone* seems to want to be a zombie!

John Amplas, zombie recruiter
for *Dawn of the Dead*
circa 1980s

It's a very conservative company and they would be very upset if everyone knew they spent their time packaging the smell of farts.

> John Waters on the company
> that made the Odorama cards
> for *Polyester*
> *1981*

I put the A camera in the most orthodox positions, use the B camera for quick, decisive shots, and the C camera as a kind of guerrilla unit.

> Akira Kurosawa on filming
> with three cameras
> *1982*

His [Dustin Hoffman's] twenty-seven-inch waist was his crowning glory and helped us feminize him.

> Ruth Morley, costume
> designer on *Tootsie*
> *1982*

We shaved his legs, his arms, and the backs of his fingers. . . . We consulted a female impersonator about his figure. . . . He's got to wear a latex-base makeup that's murder on his skin and only lasts for a few hours. It's been a nightmare trying to keep him looking like a woman.

> Sidney Pollack on Dustin
> Hoffman in *Tootsie*
> *1982*

I wanted a much more gentle score for *Jaws* . . . a kind of haunting piano. John [Williams] looked at me and said, "Hey, this is a scary pirate movie." And he came up with that bump-bum-bum-bum-bum . . . you know. A really primal, scary, Stravinsky-type of noise.

Steven Spielberg

1982

Why would I concern myself with their underwear at all? Because it helps an actor to feel a certain thing, and whatever an actor is feeling should finally affect the audience. You give Julie Christie [in *Shampoo*] an uplifted bra with pads underneath and it makes her a whole other person; this lady probably buys her underwear at places like Frederick's of Hollywood.

Anthea Sylbert, costume designer

circa 1983

Cinema [is] a generous art form. . . . Everything seems more interesting on film than in life. . . . The camera heightens reality.

Nestor Almendros, cinematographer

circa 1984

Making movies is boring. You can write it down, but no one will believe it.

Hume Cronyn

1984

The first thing I put down on paper was the image of the motorcycle I would drive. I wanted to make it attractive to people, like a red-white-and-blue cock.

> Peter Fonda on *Easy Rider*
> *circa 1984*

Steven Spielberg kept wanting more and more snakes, but he had to make do with 6,000 garden and grass snakes flown in from Holland, and used bits of garden hose to fill the spaces the boas and pythons couldn't.

> Harrison Ford on *Raiders of the Lost Ark*
> *circa 1984*

Sometimes I think the most difficult part of being in films is being cool as an airplane rolls over your leg—and acting like it doesn't hurt at all.

> Harrison Ford on a near-accident in *Raiders of the Lost Ark*
> *circa 1984*

The stunt that gets the most people hurt in this industry is the simple fight routine. . . . There are a lot of stuntmen who just cringe when they find out they've got to do a fight with an actor who's not had a lot of experience doing them—'cause nine times out of ten, they're going to get hit!

> Glen Randall, stunt coordinator
> *circa 1984*

It's tremendous fun rehearsing a fight with Sean [Connery] —you know, he's not very interested in the rehearsal and wants to get on with it; meanwhile he's punching the stuntman, who's spitting out his teeth. He'll say, "Oh, sorry, I hope I didn't hurt you."

> Guy Hamilton
> *1980*

Anything that can help the actor must be done. Little things. . . . For an Italian kitchen, which we created in *The Godfather*, you'd have to go in and mash garlic all over the place, take tomato paste and throw it on the floor, and mop it up so you'd have a little bit of last month's tomato paste spillings.

> Dean Tavoularis, art director
> *circa 1984*

We can't cater to a handful of people who know Paris. . . . Whatever you put there, they'll believe that's how it is.

> Irving Thalberg to MGM art director Cedric Gibbons, calling for an ocean in Paris
> *circa 1925*

Science Fiction and Horror

They [Karloff's eyes] mirrored the suffering of the poor dumb creature, in contrast to his frightful appearance and hideous strength.

> Carl Laemmle, Universal
> studio head, on the monster in
> *Frankenstein*
> *circa 1930s*

Hyde is not evil; he is the primitive, the animal in us. . . . Hyde is the Neanderthal man, and [Fredric] March's makeup was designed as such.

> Rouben Mamoulian on the
> 1932 *Dr. Jekyll and Mr. Hyde*
> *circa 1930s*

Karloff's face fascinated me. I made drawings of his head, added sharp bony ridges where I imagined the skull might have joined. His physique was weaker than I could wish, but that queer, penetrating personality of his, I felt, was more important than his shape.

> James Whale, director, on
> preparations for *Frankenstein*
> *circa 1930s*

The monster was inarticulate, helpless, and tragic, but I owe everything to him. He's my best friend.

> Boris Karloff
>> *circa 1960s*

I write novels for a living, and when RKO was looking for producers, someone told them I had written horrible novels. They mistook the word *horrible* for *horror* and I got the job.

> Val Lewton on how he became involved in horror films
>> *circa 1940s*

Our theme is that peace is no longer a four-letter word.

> Julian C. Blaustein, Twentieth Century-Fox producer, on the story that became *The Day the Earth Stood Still*
>> 1949

Julian [Blaustein] and I were thinking that they weren't going to make our picture because this was no time to be making a "peace" film. . . . [Darryl F. Zanuck] said, "To hell with it! Let's go ahead anyway. It's a good piece of entertainment. I believe in it."

> Edmund H. North, screenwriter, on making *The Day the Earth Stood Still* at the outbreak of the Korean War
>> 1975

The great thing about this is that it won't cost you a cent to make the monsters. You could have a thousand of them!

> Irving Block, writer, selling
> the idea of the invisible
> monster in *Forbidden Planet*
> to MGM
>
> *1954*

When you stood at one end of the stage after the backing was completed, you almost couldn't believe you were on a stage. You had to walk right up to it to believe it was background.

> George Folsey,
> cinematographer, on the 350-
> foot cyclorama depicting the
> surface of Altair IV in
> *Forbidden Planet*
>
> *1975*

When I was making *Psycho*, Paramount made for me a whole torso out of rubber for the shower scene. When one plunged a knife in it, blood would spurt out. Oh, it was wonderful. But I wouldn't use it. That would have been too simple.

> Alfred Hitchcock
>
> *circa 1960s*

Poor old Bela [Lugosi], it was a strange thing. He was really a shy, sensitive, talented man who had a fine career on the classical stage in Europe. But he made a fatal mistake. He never took the trouble to learn our language.

> Boris Karloff
>
> *circa 1960s*

Actually there was a tough-looking fellow working on the Toho lot with the nickname Gojira. We just used *his* name. It certainly fitted well.

> Eiji Tsuburaya, special effects man, on the origin of the name "Gojira," aka "Godzilla"
>
> *1964*

The trial scene [in *Planet of the Apes*] involves, as so many of my parts seem to, another manhandling. . . . They're trying to think of a different way of tying me up from those used in *Ten Commandments, Ben-Hur,* etc., etc., etc.

> Charlton Heston
>
> *1967*

People eating people. Ha! That's funny, George! That's a joke, right?

> Rudy Ricci, George A. Romero associate, on hearing Romero's idea for *Night of the Living Dead*
>
> *1967*

YOU MADE ME DREAM EYES WIDE OPEN STOP YOURS IS MUCH MORE THAN AN EXTRAORDINARY FILM THANK YOU

> Franco Zeffirelli to Stanley Kubrick on *2001: A Space Odyssey*
>
> *circa 1968*

THE MAN IN LINCOLN'S NOSE

I just made a deal with George [Lucas] for the biggest movie ever made. It's about these Wookies and this robot called C-3PO.

> Alan Ladd, Jr., production
> executive at Twentieth
> Century-Fox
>
> *1973*

"I think I just ran over a Wookie back there."
"What's a Wookie?"
"I don't know; I just made it up."
"That's great; I love that word. I'm going to use that."

> Terry McGovern and George
> Lucas
>
> *circa 1970s*

The title *Star Wars* was an insurance policy. . . . We calculated that there are something like $8 million worth of science fiction freaks in the U.S.A. and they will go to see absolutely anything with a title like *Star Wars*.

> George Lucas
>
> *circa 1978*

I've lost count of the times I've killed Christopher Lee.

> Les Bowie, special effects
> man, on Hammer's *Dracula*
> series
>
> *circa 1974*

She smokes heavy. It sounds like she has three or four different screaming animals in her throat.

>William Friedkin on
>Mercedes McCambridge, who
>did the voice of the demon in
>*The Exorcist*
>
>*1974*

The set burned down. . . . Sprinkler systems used to explode and drown the set. Just your average supernatural thing.

>William Friedkin on
>mysterious problems during
>filming of *The Exorcist*
>
>*1974*

What I thought was quite delicious [in *Invasion of the Body Snatchers*] was our playing with the fact that as a pod you don't feel any passion. So, when he comes back to the cave and she falls, he tries to kiss her awake in a delicious non-pod way, but she's a limp fish, and he knows immediately that she is a pod.

>Don Siegel
>
>*circa 1974*

Good God, it's science fiction. Why are they offering me this?

>Alec Guinness on first
>receiving the script of *Star
>Wars*
>
>*1975*

You can type this shit, George, but you sure can't say it.

> Harrison Ford to George
> Lucas on the dialogue in *Star
> Wars*
> *circa 1976*

You had to do something with the hero. You couldn't let him just disappear. That would be nothing. I wanted to say, "There are universes within universes." And I don't think that was inconsistent with the story.

> Richard Matheson,
> screenwriter, on the ending of
> *The Incredible Shrinking Man*
> *1976*

When it was released, I wasn't even the star. The story was.

> Grant Williams, star of *The
> Incredible Shrinking Man*
> *circa 1979*

I described the scene of some lady who goes into a pond and sees the corpse of a little child and gets axed to death. Everything I knew Roger would like.

> Francis Ford Coppola on
> suggesting the plot of his first
> feature film, *Dementia 13*, to
> Roger Corman
> *circa 1978*

If we have enough action, nobody will notice.

> George Lucas on lack of depth
> in *The Empire Strikes Back*
> *circa 1978*

SCIENCE FICTION AND HORROR

My first concept of the mother ship [in *Close Encounters of the Third Kind*] was terrible. It was a black, pie-shaped wedge, with a little tip on the end; a phantom shape that blotted out the stars. . . . Then I said to myself, "What am I leading up to, a Sara Lee pie tin in the third act of my movie? After all that's gone before, a black wedge is going to offer cosmic bliss?"

Steven Spielberg

circa 1978

I was really curious about what the inside of the mother ship was like, myself—I wanted to see it. So . . . I built it.

Steven Spielberg on *Close Encounters of the Third Kind: The Special Edition*

1982

Why is it such a crime for me to spend money when they can spend it for a movie about a big gorilla or some jerk who flies around in the sky?

Francis Ford Coppola on *Superman* and the remake of *King Kong*

1979

That cape was a bitch.

Richard Donner on getting Superman's cape in the 1978 film to flutter

1979

Just because I'm showing somebody being disemboweled doesn't mean I have to get heavy with a message.

> George A. Romero
> *circa 1979*

Jack Pierce was, you might say, very sentimental. When he created a live beauty makeup, he felt about it like a woman feels about her children.

> Elsa Lanchester on the man who did the makeup for her role in *The Bride of Frankenstein*
> *circa 1980*

Follow the Force.

> Mark Hamill's signature line on autographed stills from *Return of the Jedi*
> *circa 1982*

Force yourself.

> Harrison Ford's signature line
> *circa 1982*

All I knew about his appearance was that he had to be smaller than the children and as ugly as possible.

> Melissa Mathison, screenwriter on *E.T.*
> *circa 1983*

Taking the scissors, I cut out the eyes of Carl Sandburg and pasted them over the face of a small child. And I remember saying to myself, "That is weird!"

> Steven Spielberg on the
> design of E.T.
> *circa 1983*

E.T. itself was one of the dullest characters ever: He never said anything of consequence; he had no humor—nothing. I think he was just made up to look like Menachem Begin. With as much humor.

> Julius J. Epstein, screenwriter
> *1983*

When things are going the way they are in *Blade Runner*, there doesn't seem time for a bath and a shave. I think that kind of detail goes to make up the character.

> Harrison Ford on the unkempt
> appearance he insisted on in
> the film
> *circa 1984*

David [Lynch] decided he didn't want to do a George Lucas movie. Because he felt he couldn't be constantly answering to another producer. . . . Ironically, David left to make *Dune* for Dino De Laurentiis.

> Mark Hamill on why David
> Lynch didn't accept the job of
> directing *Return of the Jedi*
> *circa 1984*

I'm glad I did it. I'm glad I did all three of them. But . . .
I'm glad . . . I don't . . . have to do any more.

> Harrison Ford on *Star Wars*
> and its sequels
> *circa 1983*

I'd love to have the project of redesigning the human body.
It would please me to no end. Well—I do it in my movies.

> David Cronenberg
> *1986*

I think we automatically get along because we're both guys
who live somewhere in the middle, avoiding New York and
L.A. We both can sit and giggle at the most gruesome
sights. . . . We both like a funky, flat-out, unapologetic ap-
proach to horror. . . . a plain old steak on the coals, maybe a
little salt and pepper . . . no A-1, no Worcestershire, and
heaven forbid, no bean sprouts or avocado.

> George A. Romero on
> collaborating with Stephen
> King on *Creepshow*
> *circa 1986*

Freddy's like Shecky Greene with claws now.

> Wes Craven of the *Nightmare
> on Elm Street* sequels
> *1988*

Maybe, but I'm more of a medievalist.

> David Cronenberg on
> assertions that *Dead Ringers*
> is a throwback to the
> nineteenth century
>
> *1988*

Screenwriters

I don't like Hollywood, I don't like you, and I certainly don't like this putrid piece of Gorgonzola somebody gave me to read.

> Jo Swerling, screenwriter, to
> Harry Cohn, on the first draft
> of *Ladies of Leisure*
> *circa 1930*

Ah don't believe Ah know which pictures are yours. Do you make the Mickey Mouse brand?

> William Faulkner to Irving
> Thalberg of MGM
> *circa 1930s*

I've got America's best writer for $300 a week.

> Jack L. Warner on signing
> William Faulkner
> *circa 1930s*

This might have been good for a picture—except it has too many characters in it.

> Wilson Mizner, screenwriter,
> on the Los Angeles telephone
> directory
>> *circa 1930s*

"What's all this business about being a writer? It's just putting one word after another."
"Pardon me, Mr. Thalberg; it's putting one *right* word after another."

> Irving Thalberg and Lenore
> Coffee, screenwriter
>> *circa 1930s*

You guys can't find an ending to your story because you got no story in the *first* place.

> Jules Furthman, screenwriter,
> on *Meet John Doe*
>> *circa 1940*

They were treated much like butlers, socially.

> Ben Hecht on the status of
> screenwriters
>> *circa 1940s*

The screenwriter is the highest-paid secretary in the world.

> Joseph L. Mankiewicz
>> *1940s*

Jim, I'm delighted with what you've done. But *she* couldn't play your dialogue. It has to be translated into the kind of baby talk she can handle.

> George Waggner to James M.
> Cain, on Maria Montez's
> needs in *Gypsy Wildcat*
> *circa 1943*

I don't know how it is that you start working at something you don't like, and before you know it, you're an old man.

> Herman J. Mankiewicz on
> writing for the movies
> *circa 1953*

Nor is movie writing easier than good writing. It's just as hard to make a toilet seat as it is a castle window. But the view is different.

> Ben Hecht
> *1957*

Let me tell you about writing for films. You finish your book. Now, you know where the California state line is? Well, you drive right up to that line, take your manuscript, and pitch it across— No, on second thought, don't pitch it across. First, let them toss the money over. *Then* you throw it over, pick up the money, and get the hell out of there.

> Ernest Hemingway during
> pre-production for *The Old
> Man and the Sea*
> *circa 1957*

Hemingway and I were fishing down in Key West, and I was trying to get him to write for movies. . . . I said, "Look, you're broke all the time. Why the deuce don't you make some money? Anything you write you can make into a movie. I can make a movie out of the worst thing you ever wrote." He said, "What's the worst thing I ever wrote?" I said, "That piece of junk called *To Have and Have Not*."

Howard Hawks

circa 1970s

The fledgling New Yorkers were easily spotted by their superior, "slumming" attitudes—endemic to all East Coast writers who came to Hollywood.

Frank Capra

1971

The Hacketts [Albert Hackett and Frances Goodrich] were writing some bright, sensitive scenes, but why didn't the scenes move me? I sat down and wrote some key scenes. . . . Take it or leave it—things had to be done my way.

Frank Capra on *It's a Wonderful Life*

1971

"We never stayed on the thing all the way [*It's a Wonderful Life*]."
"Not for that horrid man [Frank Capra]."
"He's a very arrogant son of a bitch. . . . We've never seen the thing."
"It's the only unpleasant experience we've ever had."

Albert Hackett and Frances Goodrich on writing *It's a Wonderful Life*

1983

Ben [Hecht] was always good at pressure jobs. He worked on *Gone With the Wind* for David Selznick—never read *that* either. Claimed reading the book would only confuse him.

Leland Hayward
circa 1971

I remember we bought [John Steinbeck's] *The Moon Is Down*, which was on stage in New York, and when I said, "Look, have you got any suggestions?" he [Steinbeck] said, "Yeah, tamper with it."

Nunnally Johnson
circa 1971

[S. J. Perelman] always disclaimed working on the pictures, because he wanted to show that he was a real high-class writer and wouldn't deign to work on anything like a Marx Brothers film. But when we became very successful, then he claimed he wrote everything!

Groucho Marx
circa 1973

I do know that the boys [Julius J. and Philip G. Epstein] wrote the police stuff and the comedy [in *Casablanca*], and they wrote it very well. . . . So what it came to was I wrote the love story. I wrote the scene where she came to him, the scene where the husband comes to Rick, and the finish of the thing.

Casey Robinson
1974

Listen, he [Hal B. Wallis] had seventy-five writers trying to come up with an ending [to *Casablanca*]. Everybody in the studio was trying to come up with an ending. They were panic-stricken. . . . [Then] my brother [Philip G. Epstein] and I . . . were driving to the studio and that's when we thought of the ending.

> Julius J. Epstein
>
> *1983*

Roosevelt and Churchill had just met in Casablanca, and the order came down from Jack Warner that *Casablanca* would finish with the conference between Roosevelt and Churchill! How we got out of that I don't know.

> Casey Robinson
>
> *1974*

I don't hate it. I just think it was slick shit.

> Julius J. Epstein on
> *Casablanca*, one of his
> projects
>
> *1983*

We [William Goldman and director Alan Pakula] would meet and discuss a scene—any scene, it doesn't matter—and I would ask if it was okay, and if it wasn't, how did he want it changed, what direction? For example, I might ask, did he want this shorter or longer?

He would answer, "Do it both ways, I want to see it all."

"Both ways?"

"Both ways."

I might ask, did he want me to rewrite a sequence and make it more or less hard-edged.

He would answer, "Do it both ways, I want to see it all."

"Both ways?"

"Both ways absolutely."

"But why?"

And now would come the answer that I always associate with Alan: "Don't deprive me of any riches."

> William Goldman on his role
> as screenwriter for *All the
> President's Men*
> *circa 1975*

I must say Billy Wilder did a terrific job [on *Double Indemnity*]. It's the only picture I ever saw made from my books that had things in it I wish I had thought of. Wilder's ending was much better than my ending, and his device for letting the guy tell the story by taking out the office dictating machine —I would have done it if I had thought of it.

> James M. Cain
> *circa 1976*

Somebody told me about it [the Hitchcock/Truffaut interview], and he said, "Do you realize what Hitchcock said about you in that book?" . . . [Truffaut] says, "Didn't John Michael Hayes do *Rear Window*?" . . . [Hitchcock] answered, "Oh yes, he was just a radio writer I brought in to work on the dialogue." Mr. Hitchcock knew very well that I had already been a screenwriter. It's like saying, "David Sarnoff was a newspaper boy—oh ya, I just took a newspaper boy and put him in charge of RCA."

> John Michael Hayes
> *circa 1978*

Everything Hitchcock says is always his conception. The one thing Hitch has never allowed for is for any writer to have any real credit. It always has to be Hitch.

> Charles Bennett
> *circa 1985*

I wanted Ben Hecht to write on it [*Scarface*], and he said, "Sure, what are you going to make?" I said, "A gangster picture." He said, "Hell, you don't want to make one of those things." I said, "Well, Ben, I've got an idea that the Borgia family is living in Chicago today. See, our Borgia is Al Capone, and his sister does the same incest thing as Lucretia Borgia." And he said, "Well, let's start tomorrow morning."

Howard Hawks

circa 1931

Ben [Hecht] said that to [Howard] *Hawks*. I heard him say that. The Borgias have always been Ben's favorite characters. Howard, bless his heart, probably knew who they were, but I think he looked them up in the encyclopedia.

John Lee Mahin,
screenwriter, on the Borgia
allusion in *Scarface*

1979

Howard [Hawks] was such a liar! . . . Like he said he invented the nickel thing [in *Scarface*]. He didn't at all. It was all in the script. . . . [George] Raft flips a nickel constantly, nervously. I can remember the way Ben [Hecht] said, "He flips a nickel nervously."

John Lee Mahin

circa 1979

You know that coin thing in *Scarface*? . . . That was [George] Raft's idea.

W. R. Burnett, screenwriter
circa 1982

Writing is more fun than anything else, because nothing can go wrong that can hurt you; you're just locked in at home.

Woody Allen

circa 1980

It's one thing to send a script to actors and *imagine* how they sound reading your wonderful lines for the first time, but when you actually hear those lines being read aloud, it's like taking a cold shower.

Woody Allen

circa 1980

He'd be great unless he started being Groucho *at* me.

Norman Krasna on
collaborating on screenplays
with Groucho Marx

circa 1980

[Ian Fleming said] to me once, "The pictures are much funnier than my books." He was a little bemused and a little obtuse about it . . . because he really didn't understand that we were *trying* to make them funnier.

Richard Maibaum,
screenwriter on several Bond
films

circa 1980s

The only one who gets screwed around with basically is the writer, because, as I say, everybody knows the alphabet. And the producer makes contributions, and so does the actor's mistress, and so does the agent, and all that.

William Goldman

circa 1982

For truly cinematic expression, the camera and the microphone must be able to cross both fire and water. That is what makes a real movie. The script must be something that has the power to do this.

Akira Kurosawa

1982

On *The Godfather*, Francis [Ford Coppola] was perplexed. In the book there wasn't any resolution between Vito Corleone and his son Michael. . . . Francis kept saying, "Well, I want the audience to know that they love each other." He put it that way. But you couldn't do a scene about two people loving each other. So I wrote a scene about the succession of power, and *through* that it was obvious that the two men had a great deal of affection for each other. . . . It's illustrative in a way of writing in general. Most scenes are rarely about what the subject matter is.

Robert Towne

circa 1982

We thought of everyone as being homosexual, so we never had to worry about that.

Albert Hackett on whether
male or female characters
were easier to write

1983

In the middle-thirties, in American films, a horrible thing happened; every line had to be a quip of some sort. Every damned line. Like someone would say, "I won't forget you," and someone else would reply, "I've forgotten you already."

Charles Bennett
circa 1985

One of the first things you had to learn was to not let them break your heart.

Donald Ogden Stewart
circa 1985

I did mix my blood with *The Fly.*

David Cronenberg on
collaborating with
screenwriter Charles Pogue
1986

Savored among old-time screenwriters is the apocryphal story of how Robert Riskin, the writer of *Lady for a Day, It Happened One Night, Mr. Deeds Goes to Town, Lost Horizon,* and other "Capracorn," entered the director's office in a fury, threw 120 blank pages of script on his desk, and announced, "Here! Let's see you give *that* the Capra touch!"

Pat McGilligan, film critic
1986

Sex Appeal

You know Mr. [D. W.] Griffith told us we must *never* kiss actors—it isn't healthy.

> Dorothy Gish to a director
> requesting a kissing scene
> *circa 1915*

Doing such things before the camera! How can I compete with that?

> D. W. Griffith on hearing of a
> scene in which a woman takes
> off her stockings in *Wildflower*
> *circa 1920*

You can't be much of a glamour girl with chipmunk cheeks.

> Joan Blondell on her looks
> *circa 1930s*

Edith, I'm a lady, but most of all I'm a sexy female. . . . I want my clothes loose enough to prove I'm a lady, but tight enough to show 'em I'm a woman.

> Mae West to costume designer
> Edith Head
> *circa 1930s*

In seeing Clark Gable tonight in this picture I think we should definitely have [contract player] Lyle Talbot grow a mustache just like his. It gives him a sort of flash and good looks.

> Jack L. Warner on seeing
> Gable in *It Happened One
> Night*
>
> *1934*

[Gregory] Peck we know to be the new rage, and if any further proof were needed, it was to be found . . . at the pre-views of *Spellbound*. We could not keep the audience quiet from the time his name first came on the screen until we had shushed the audience through three or four sequences and stopped all the dames from "oohing" and "aahing" and gur-gling.

> David O. Selznick
>
> *1945*

Mr. [Darryl F.] Zanuck feels that you may turn into an ac-tress sometime, but that your type of looks is definitely against you.

> Twentieth Century-Fox
> casting official to Marilyn
> Monroe
>
> *circa 1940s*

I saw she was one of those blondes who put on ten years if you take a close look at them.

> Marilyn Monroe on Zsa Zsa
> Gabor
>
> *circa 1950s*

They both smiled at me as if I were a piece of French pastry.

> Marilyn Monroe on meeting
> Groucho and Harpo Marx
> *circa 1950s*

Sometimes I've been to a party where no one spoke to me a whole evening. The men, frightened by their wives or sweeties, would give me a wide berth. And the ladies would gang up in a corner to discuss my dangerous character.

> Marilyn Monroe
> *circa 1950s*

Him? I thought he was one of the guys from the building—you know, the guys that fix things.

> Joseph E. Levine, producer,
> on meeting Dustin Hoffman,
> chosen for the lead in *The Graduate*
> *circa 1966*

Hey, now, listen. If actors have to work nude, and they're embarrassed about it, it should be union rules that the crew be nude, too, and then nobody will be staring at anybody.

> Jack Nicholson on the set of
> *Five Easy Pieces*
> *circa 1969*

If you have sex, you don't have to be conscious of it. . . . If you don't have it, well, any cow can act it, but it shows through.

> Mae West
> *circa 1969*

I have always been the brunette who lost out, and I've always gotten the wrong end of everything! I've gone through all my life without a single diamond!

> Anita Loos, author of the
> novel *Gentlemen Prefer
> Blondes*
>
> *1965*

Ann Sheridan walked in and they said, "That's the 'Oomph' Girl." I said, "Excuse me," and went up to my room to look in my dictionary to see what "oomph" meant.

> Ingrid Bergman
>
> *1972*

I saw *The Last Picture Show*. I thought if one more person stripped slowly, I would go crazy.

> Marlene Dietrich to Peter
> Bogdanovich
>
> *circa 1973*

Fred [Astaire] is so sensitive about everything. You know, it took me three years to get Fred to kiss a girl on the screen. On the lips.

> Arthur Freed
>
> *1974*

On the first take, Jack got a little crazy with me and whipped me into a venetian blind, which is very sharp if you hit it that fast, and it cut my leg. . . . The second time, Jack lost his balance and went through a plate-glass window and cut his hand open horribly. . . . The third take we got it.

> Sally Struthers on her love
> scene with Jack Nicholson in
> *Five Easy Pieces*
> *circa 1975*

Great legs and tight buttocks, a real great seat, and small, sensitive feet.

> Katharine Hepburn on John
> Wayne
> *1979*

All that crap comes from the way I walk. There's evidently a virility in it, otherwise why do you keep mentioning it?

> John Wayne on his alleged
> sexiness
> *1971*

I would never say that the sarong made Dorothy Lamour a star. If someone else had worn it, chances are that neither the girl nor the sarong would have been heard of again. But when Dottie filled out that piece of cloth, it was magic.

> Edith Head, costume designer
> *circa 1980*

I learned my restraint lessons very well. In what was one of the sexiest love scenes ever on the screen [in *Notorious*], [Ingrid] Bergman and [Cary] Grant were totally dressed, but who remembers what they wore?

> Edith Head
> *circa 1980*

Marilyn [Monroe] was a free spirit who should have been dressed in such a way that she would be able to forget about her clothes. When a woman is sexy, she knows it and she doesn't need clothes that constantly remind her.

Edith Head

circa 1980

I've never felt like a terrific lover on screen or in private. You know what it was to be out here in Hollywood? Christ. . . . [There'd] be Tyrone Power at one table with a knockout of a girl, and Bob Taylor at another table with Barbara Stanwyck. Those guys gave me a complex. They *looked* like lovers! Sure I had to kiss girls in pictures, Bette Davis, Barbara Stanwyck, Joan Crawford, Joan Bennett, but I wasn't any good at it.

Henry Fonda

1982

Hank [Henry Fonda] will refuse to admit the truth. . . . [Joan Crawford] found Fonda very attractive. When ordinary approaches failed to get a reaction from him, she asked the wardrobe department to make a jockstrap of rhinestones, gold sequins, and red beads. Crawford gave the package to Henry on the set [of *Daisy Kenyon*] one morning, gift-wrapped.

Dore Schary

circa 1980

They had a can of stuff they called "Sex." It was Vaseline, and you rubbed it on your shoulders to make them gleam . . . and, oh my God, really you felt ridiculous. But what were you going to do? It was, "Wet your lips, honey, and suck in your tummy and look sultry and think a smile."

Anne Baxter

circa 1980s

Richard [Gere] has become a big star based on his attraction for women. He's got a pinup image—which he *hates*, and I understand that. The only trouble is, whenever they ask him to take his trousers off, he does.

Michael Caine

1983

I'm developing a love story where you can actually see a man and a woman kissing in one of my movies.

Steven Spielberg

circa 1983

When I first made the sketch [of Warren Beatty's leather jacket in *Shampoo*], I made a mistake: I put zippers on the jacket. We started to make it, and I started to think that zippers are not really sexy, because . . . they are keeping me from seeing his body as well as I want to see it. . . . Even the jeans —we started off by just buying jeans; after all, jeans are jeans. Well, you couldn't see his body well enough, so we custom-made the jeans. His shirts were silk. Everything he wore had some kind of sexuality to it.

Anthea Sylbert, costume designer

circa 1983

Nobody can be petted, touched, and kissed without feeling something.

> Kathleen Turner on playing
> sex scenes in movies
> *1986*

It was very, very hot stuff. . . . After we finished the break-in scene in the house, I ran to my dressing room and I was shaking and crying and I sort of broke down. I did that after almost every one of those heavy scenes.

> Kathleen Turner on one of the
> sex scenes in *Body Heat*
> *1986*

He's the best kisser I ever met in the movies.

> Meryl Streep on Robert
> Redford
> *circa 1988*

Silent Films

We've found a universal language—a power that can make men brothers and end war forever. Remember that. Remember that when you stand in front of a camera!

> D. W. Griffith to his cast
> before each movie
> *circa 1910*

"We got us a spectacle, kids. Bauman and Kessel are always hollering about costs. Look at that crowd scene—all free!"
"What's the story, boss?"
"Got no story. We'll make it up as we go along."

> Mack Sennett and Henry
> "Pathé" Lehrman,
> encountering a Shriners'
> parade in Los Angeles
> *circa 1912*

We will bury ourselves in hard work out at the coast for five years and make the greatest pictures ever made, make a million dollars, and retire, and then you can have all the time you want to fool around with your camera gadgets.

> D. W. Griffith coaxing
> cameraman Billy Bitzer to join
> his independent company
> *circa 1913*

When an actor feels the character he is playing, the "close-up" is an invaluable asset. If it is a tense scene . . . then, despite all rules of technique to the contrary, I claim that the scene demands a "close-up" of the actor's face cut quickly into the main scene.

> William S. Hart, silent screen
> actor
> *1917*

Your refusal to face the world is making you more and more a sentimentalist. You see passion in terms of cooing doves or the falling of a rose petal. . . . Your lack of contact with life makes you deficient in humor. . . . Your splendid unsophistication is a menace to you—and to pictures.

> James R. Quirk in a *Photoplay*
> editorial addressed to D. W.
> Griffith
> *1924*

I remember one old film in which there suddenly flashed across the screen a title: Then He Went to London. There was no occasion in the story why he should go to London and no one knew who he was. . . . The only possible reason for this journey was that they happened to have around the studio an

English joke or gag which they thought would prove irresistible on the screen.

Buster Keaton

1926

Once I was lured into attending the opening of a new theater in Philadelphia. . . . I heard someone say: "Stick a pin in him, and see if you can make him laugh." It was with no little apprehension and a great deal of effort that I reached a cab outside the station.

Buster Keaton

1926

We had the train picture, *The Black Diamond Express.* . . . Here were six or seven thousand people who had never seen a motion picture before, and when that train came right at them on the screen, they were amazed, with me behind making the "choo, choo, choo" and the bell and noises of a train. . . . [T]hey went into a real panic and the first twenty rows of seats were emptied . . . and one woman went out screaming and they never saw her afterwards.

J. Stuart Blackton, director

1929

When we were boys, a friend and I walked downtown to this nickelodeon. . . . Inside we laughed ourselves into stitches, not at how good the jokes were but at how awful they were. . . . The feature was *The Great Train Robbery.* I had no idea that this was moving picture history. To us it was utterly beyond belief, it was so lousy. We came out agreeing it was *not* good entertainment, but it passed the time.

James M. Cain, screenwriter

circa 1976

There never was a *silent* film. We'd finish a picture, show it in one of our projection rooms, and come out shattered. It would be awful.... Then we'd show it in a theater, with a girl down in the pit pounding away at a piano, and there would be all the difference in the world. Without that music, there wouldn't have been a movie industry at all.

Irving Thalberg

circa 1930s

Movies were seldom written. In 1927 they were yelled into existence in conferences that kept going in saloons, brothels, and all-night poker games.

Ben Hecht

1954

We would work, say, Monday, Tuesday, and Wednesday shooting and make two pictures. Then on Thursday and Friday I'd develop and cut them and take Saturday and Sunday off.

Allan Dwan

circa 1970

We always knew the dialogue would be changed, because they had special writers for that. I'd play a love scene with a girl and I'd say, "Oh gee, you're not looking so good. Where did you go last night?" and the caption writer would change that to, "Darling, you look beautiful."

Charles "Buddy" Rogers
circa 1980s

The infant industry has taken the ribbons from her hair. She has put away some of her bright toys—she is growing up. She may have a child, one day, and the child's name may be Television, but that's another story.

> Edmund Goulding, director,
> on the coming of sound
>> *1928*

I wasn't afraid of sound. I knew I could talk.

> Bebe Daniels, actress
>> *1969*

It really was just like *Singin' in the Rain.*

> Walter Plunkett, costume
> designer, on the transition to
> sound
>> *circa 1969*

I can remember vividly how tough it was on actors and actresses when the silent pictures gave way to talkies.... There was a fire one day at Paramount, and Clara Bow ran out screaming, "I hope to Christ it was the sound stages!"

> Joseph L. Mankiewicz
>> *circa 1971*

They had no sound stages, so they stripped the props department of miles of carpeting and used that to line the walls of the silent stages.

> Joseph L. Mankiewicz on the
> transition to sound at
> Paramount
>> *circa 1980s*

It was that serious that [Gary] Cooper and Dick Arlen and Jack Oakie and I made a pledge that if one of us didn't have a voice, we'd each give 10 percent of our salaries to him as long as we lived.

> Buddy Rogers on the
> transition to sound
>
> *circa 1980s*

Swashbucklers and Epics

The littlest thing . . . is the sigh of General Lee as the papers of surrender were signed.

> D. W. Griffith on the
> importance of small details in
> *The Birth of a Nation*
> *1915*

What do you want me to do, stop shooting and release it as *The Five Commandments*?

> Cecil B. De Mille responding
> to charges of overspending
> *circa 1922*

It was a theory that died very hard that the public would not stand for anyone dressed in clothes of another period. . . . I got around this objection by staging what we call a vision. The poor working girl was dreaming of love and reading *Tristan and Isolde*. The scene faded out, and scenes were depicted on the screen that the girl was supposed to be reading. . . . Thus a bit of a costume picture was put over on the man who bought the picture for his theater, and there was no protest from the public.

> Cecil B. De Mille
> *1927*

I always had to do what that conceited old goat wanted, whether it was correct or not. He never did an authentic costume picture in his entire career.

>   Edith Head on Cecil B.
>   De Mille
>   *circa 1980*

In selecting the actors for *The King of Kings* I was guided by the principle that the greatest story ought to have the greatest cast possible. Some of my associates think that I have misspelled a word and that what I really meant was the greatest "cost."

>   Cecil B. De Mille
>   *1927*

Louis, forget it. No Civil War picture ever made a nickel.

>   Irving Thalberg to Louis B.
>   Mayer, on hearing about *Gone
>   With the Wind*
>   *circa 1930s*

Don't you think that [James] Cagney would make a swell Robin Hood?

>   Dwight Franklin, Warner
>   Bros. visual consultant, to Jack
>   L. Warner
>   *1935*

I don't understand what you can be thinking about at times. . . . Instead of playing that [scene in *Captain Blood*] in a close-up . . . of Errol Flynn . . . you play it in a long shot so that you can get the composition of a candlestick and a wine bottle on a table in the foreground, which I don't give a damn about. . . . Please don't forget that the most important thing you have to do is to get the story on the screen. . . . If you don't have a story, all of the composition shots and all the candles in the world aren't going to make you a good picture.

> Hal B. Wallis to director
> Michael Curtiz
>
> *1935*

I distinctly remember telling you, I don't know how many times, that I did not want you to use lace collars or cuffs on Errol Flynn [in *Captain Blood*]. . . . I want the man to look like a pirate, not a mollycoddle.

> Hal B. Wallis to director
> Michael Curtiz
>
> *1935*

In our picture [*Gone With the Wind*] I think we have to be awfully careful that the Negroes come out decidedly on the right side of the ledger.

> David O. Selznick
>
> *1937*

I have reluctantly, and at long last, come to the conclusion that we have simply got to do something, and promptly, about the Cukor situation. I have thought that George was a great asset to the company, but I am fearful that he is, on the contrary, a very expensive luxury.

> David O. Selznick advocating
> George Cukor's dismissal
> from *Gone With the Wind*
>
> *1938*

For David Selznick, *Gone With the Wind* was the supreme effort of his career; he was enormously nervous about the whole thing. . . . It was a great trial, but also his undoing.

> George Cukor, fired from
> directing *Gone With the Wind*
> *circa 1968*

If we don't find a new Ashley [for *Gone With the Wind*], I suppose our best possibilities, depressing as it seems, are Leslie Howard and Melvyn Douglas.

> David O. Selznick
> *1938*

For your information, I am informed by MGM that Clark Gable refuses under any circumstances to have any kind of a Southern accent.

> David O. Selznick to then–
> *Gone With the Wind* director
> George Cukor
> *1938*

It would be a defiance of the laws of nature to assume that there would not be a substantial percentage of the audience who would find it necessary to go to the lavatory in the course of almost four hours of film.

> David O. Selznick on putting
> an intermission in *Gone With
> the Wind*
> *1939*

We have secured the right to use *Elizabeth and Essex*, and I have added the words, *The Private Lives of* to it. We ran into a big snag in using *The Lady and the Knight,* which I could not overcome. Furthermore, in case we both do not know, you cannot call a queen a lady.

Jack L. Warner

1939

I'd *love* to redo *Elizabeth and Essex* one more time. . . . I would feel more comfortable as the older queen. Since I *am* an older . . . queen.

Bette Davis

1974

Dear Sir: Please don't send me any more pictures where they write with feathers.

Iowa movie-theater owner
writing to MGM about
costume dramas

circa 1940s

I didn't like it. Samson had bigger tits than Delilah.

Groucho Marx on seeing
Samson and Delilah

circa 1949

I worked my ass off this morning. . . . Sixteen takes for me to say, "I'm a Jew!"

Charlton Heston during
filming of *Ben-Hur*

1958

Charioteering is a hard-won and largely useless skill, but I can't help taking pride in it.

> Charlton Heston
>
> *1958*

I just wanted to act, to have a chance to play a character, to say good-bye to the swashbuckler roles, to get swords and horses the hell out of my life.

> Errol Flynn
>
> *1959*

When we made *Dr. Zhivago* . . . we were all in Madrid in a temperature of 116 degrees, muffled up to the ears in Russian furs. We just wanted to say our lines and get out of the heat!

> Alec Guinness
>
> *circa 1960s*

"A," I'm not very good at it, and "B," I cannot imagine anyone in a costume picture ever going to the bathroom.

> Alfred Hitchcock on why he does not like to do costume films
>
> *circa 1960s*

Its Lawrence bears much the same relation to Colonel Thomas Edward Lawrence that Elizabeth Taylor's Cleopatra does to that famous lady.

> Stanley Weintraub, Lawrence biographer, on the movie *Lawrence of Arabia*
>
> *circa 1960s*

Now that would make an interesting picture.

> Anthony Mann, seeing
> Gibbon's *The Decline and
> Fall of the Roman Empire* in a
> bookstore window
> > *circa 1961*

Poor Bob Taylor, he didn't belong in that picture [*Quo Vadis*]. He's a nice boy—but we fought against it—we wanted Stewart Granger, another Englishman, or somebody who could wear those costumes; only Englishmen can wear those damned togas, speak those lines.

> John Lee Mahin
> > *circa 1978*

Now in this scene, Pete baby, it's all your fault.

> Mervyn LeRoy directing Peter
> Ustinov as Nero in the
> burning-of-Rome scene in
> *Quo Vadis*
> > *circa 1950*

[I]t was kind of fun to see if we could cook up something out of a lot of sets and costumes and characters . . . those left over from *The Robe*, those that hadn't been killed off.

> Philip Dunne on writing
> *Demetrius and the Gladiators*
> *circa 1985*

Before shooting [on *The Egyptians*] began, there wandered into my office an actor who was sort of gaunt and a strange-looking color—a very interesting fellow. He had a stage reputation. I said to myself, "My gosh, this is Akhenaten. He's the fellow for the weird epileptic emperor." . . . The actor was John Cassavetes, a wonderful Akhenaten. Zanuck, of course, cast Michael Wilding, an English comedian.

Philip Dunne
circa 1985

Some students of the cinema think that the greatest miracle achieved by C. B. [DeMille] in [the silent version of] *The Ten Commandments* was to persuade Theodore Roberts, his chief actor, whose trademark was a cigar like Ernie Kovacs's, to abandon it while he played Moses.

Michael Powell
circa 1986

I don't know how God managed. I'm having a terrible time.

John Huston during the
making of *The Bible*
circa 1965

Westerns

You may get some real good parts from this one. If this picture is half as good as I think it is, you're actually going to have to go out and buy some clothes.

> John Ford to John Wayne on
> *Stagecoach*
> *circa 1939*

If they had, it would have been the end of the picture, wouldn't it?

> John Ford on why the Indians
> didn't just shoot the horses to
> stop the coach in *Stagecoach*
> *circa 1940s*

He [John Ford] gave me a list of about fifty books to read—memoirs, novels, anything about the period. Later he sent me down into the old Apache country to nose around, get the smell and the feel of the land.... When I got back, Ford asked me if I thought I had enough research. I said yes.

"Good," he said. "Now just forget everything you've read, and we'll start writing a movie."

> Frank S. Nugent,
> screenwriter, on preparations
> for *Fort Apache*
> *circa 1947*

I never knew the big son of a bitch could act.

> John Ford to Howard Hawks
> on John Wayne's performance
> in *Red River*
> *circa 1948*

I did all the stunts myself. I wasn't a phony cowboy. . . . I never wore loud clothes, but what real cowboys wear. . . . I stuck my gun in my belt instead of in a fancy holster. I never featured a horse. . . . I never sang.

> Hoot Gibson
> *circa 1950s*

You know what we've got to do with Wyatt and Doc? We're playing two pre-Freudian fags. We're in love with each other and we don't know how to express ourselves that way—so we just kind of look at each other and grunt and don't say very much.

> Burt Lancaster to Kirk
> Douglas, on *Gunfight at the
> O.K. Corral*
> *circa 1956*

Exhibitors were absolute death on what they called "Coonskin Westerns." They were referring, of course, to Westerns

made with costumes that included the use of beaver hats. . . .
Then along came Walt Disney . . . and set the world on its ear
with *Davy Crockett,* a "Coonskin Western."

David O. Selznick

1956

Putting me in cowboy pictures seemed to me the most ridiculous miscasting. . . . I [always] had to alibi my accent . . .
[with] a couple of lines which went like this . . .
HEAVY: *Where you from, pardner?*
FLYNN: *I happen to come from Ireland, but I am as American as you are.*

Errol Flynn

1959

My name's John Ford. I make Westerns.

John Ford

circa 1960s

I knew Wyatt Earp. In the very early silent days, a couple
of times a year, he would come up to visit pals, cowboys he
knew in Tombstone; a lot of them were in my company. I
think I was an assistant prop boy then, and I used to give him
a chair and a cup of coffee, and he told me about the fight at
the O.K. Corral. So in *My Darling Clementine,* we did it exactly the way it had been. They didn't just walk up the street
and start banging away at each other; it was a clever military
maneuver.

John Ford

circa 1960s

THE MAN IN LINCOLN'S NOSE

I had one hang-up as an actor. I had no talent. I didn't hide that. I told directors that. . . . They protected me. I made the same movie twenty times.

> Audie Murphy on his Western films
> *circa 1960s*

I figured I needed a gimmick, so I dreamed up the drawl, the squint, and a way of moving which meant to suggest that I wasn't looking for trouble but would just as soon throw a bottle at your head as not.

> John Wayne
> *1962*

[John] Ford got out and stood looking around for a moment, one hand holding the cup, the other on the backside of his hip. . . . [A]s he started toward the camera, his movement was jaunty, both arms swinging, his body moving slightly from side to side—and suddenly you knew where John Wayne got his walk.

> Peter Bogdanovich
> *1967*

Well, as long as you're going to do one Western, you might as well do two.

> Roger Corman promising support to director Monte Hellman for *Ride in the Whirlwind* and *The Shooting*
> *circa 1964*

I've killed more Indians than Custer, Beecher, and Chivington put together, and people in Europe always want to know about the Indians. There are two sides to every story, but I wanted to show their point of view for a change.

> John Ford on why he made
> *Cheyenne Autumn*
> *1966*

It's the tragedy of a loner.

> John Ford on *The Searchers*
> *1966*

I thought it was pretty obvious. . . . You could tell from the way she picked up his cape, and I think you could tell from Ward Bond's expression and from his exit—as though he hadn't noticed anything.

> John Ford on whether the
> sister-in-law in *The Searchers*
> was in love with John Wayne
> *1966*

Rio Bravo was made because I didn't like a picture called *High Noon*. . . . I didn't think a good sheriff was going to go running around town like a chicken with his head off asking for help, and finally his Quaker wife had to save him.

> Howard Hawks
> *circa 1970s*

I think they felt threatened by the fact that the Western hero [in *High Noon*] was a man who was not fearless. He had enormous courage, but he was not fearless. He was afraid, and the traditionalists thought the Western hero was a man who didn't know what fear was. I always thought that was very childish.

> Fred Zinnemann
>
> *circa 1980s*

"Just came back to say good-bye, Jack."
"Good-bye, Howard. . . . Howard."
"Yes, Jack?"
"I mean *really* good-bye, Howard."
"Really good-bye, Jack?"
"Really good-bye."

> Howard Hawks and John
> Ford, shortly before Ford's
> death
>
> *1972*

Luciano [Vincenzoni] had written those movies [the spaghetti Westerns] as comedies, but Sergio [Leone] filmed them as though they were deep tragedies. This tension between the writer's and director's intentions somehow produced pictures that were quite interesting.

> Peter Bogdanovich
>
> *1973*

[William] Boyd hated the singing cowboys because he couldn't sing.

> Russell Hayden, costar, with
> Boyd, of the Hopalong
> Cassidy Westerns
>
> *circa 1976*

Hell, I wouldn't give you a dime to be a straight actor. I made four or five straight pictures, and I never liked them at all. . . . I just thought it was a hell of a lot of fun to read a couple of lines and get on a horse and ride off.

Russell Hayden
circa 1976

I'd get him to do rope tricks and show me because, well, I could rope a little, like on a ranch, but he was a magnificent roper.

Joel McCrea on Will Rogers
circa 1976

I'd like this boy to be with me on all my pictures because he'd fit.

Will Rogers on Joel McCrea
circa 1930

I did a picture once in which a woman was crossing the prairie from the East to the gold rush. She had to face a buffalo stampede, three Indian attacks, and a prairie fire. But every morning the heroine came out of the prairie schooner wearing white ruffles and her hair done up in curls. But nobody cared, because then the public accepted motion pictures only as a fantasy and an amusement.

Edith Head
circa 1980

What remains of these films in my heart is that reliable manly spirit and the smell of male sweat.

> Akira Kurosawa on William S. Hart Westerns
>
> *1982*

It takes a man who's been around horses and knows about the West. . . . These New York actors come out here from the stage and they get on the set, and suddenly they're confronted with dust and wind and tumbleweed, and the horses are rearing and snorting, and they find it's not that easy.

> Glenn Ford on what it takes to be a Western star
>
> *circa 1980s*

I've always lived out West. I've always liked the way of life, the code. And I like to go see Westerns.

> Clint Eastwood
>
> *circa 1983*

Westerns are successful throughout the world because nobody says anything.

> James Stewart
>
> *1983*